Alphonso Alva Hopkins

Geraldine

A souvenir of the St. Lawrence

Alphonso Alva Hopkins

Geraldine

A souvenir of the St. Lawrence

ISBN/EAN: 9783337233358

Printed in Europe, USA, Canada, Australia, Japan

Cover: Foto ©Andreas Hilbeck / pixelio.de

More available books at **www.hansebooks.com**

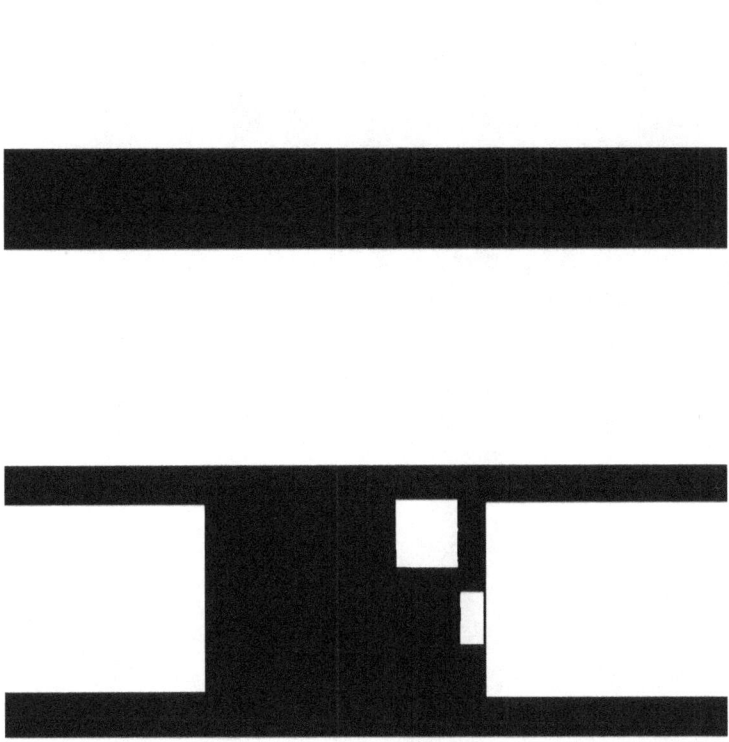

all here be N   .

PREFACE.

YEARS ago I resolved to write a romance in the style of verse which follows. I chose this style as specially well adapted to a wide variety of expression, and because at that time, so far as I knew, no author had employed it at such length and for such purpose. When it was similarly made use of by an English poet, at a date much more recent than my resolve, his poem's popularity confirmed my choice as wise; but I have refrained persistently from reading that poem, or hearing it read, or in any way learning of its character, spirit, and scope, lest unconsciously I might borrow of its style or thought. Having now taken leave, so far as probably I ever can, of my own "Geraldine," I shall devote the earliest leisure accorded me to becoming acquainted with Owen Meredith's "Lucile."

I.

THERE is something of poetry born in us each,
Though in many, perhaps, it is born without speech, —
An existence but dumb and uncertain, that strives
For expression in vain through the whole of their lives;
That is glad when the spring wears its beautiful smile,
And is sad when all nature to tears would beguile;
That can feel in the summer a glory divine
Thrilling on through the days in their silvery shine;
That can drink in delight in its radiance rare
When the mellow-hued autumn breathes peace like a
    prayer;
That can weep with the world in its woe of to-day,
And to-morrow take part in its merriest play;
That can stand on the mountain-tops often, and see
Where the far-away gardens of paradise be;
That can sound with its plummet of feeling the deeps
Where despair in the darkness of destiny sleeps;
That can feel, and can be, yet can never express

But that yearns with a yearning no poet e'er knew
In its silence of years for the speech of the few.

He was barely a poet, this friend of my verse,
Though the singers not seldom at measure are worse,
And at rhyme; for his ear was so delicate strung
That it caught the clear music, whatever was sung,
And was deaf to all discord, or listened as one
For whom time of tormenting had early begun:
He was less than a poet, if poetry means
To bewilder the senses with fanciful scenes;
To envelop each thought with such mystery round
As to leave it a marvel of meaning profound;
To make pretence of passion, and tragedy act
As if love were a lie, and all fiction were fact;
To be chiefly unreal, yet ever to seem
As if always the real came dressed in a dream.
Yet men spoke of his poems with praise, though they said,
"He is playing at verse," as delighted they read:
"He was meant for a poet in earnest, but waits
For a storm-flood of feeling to open the gates
Of his soul, till the song that is hidden shall rise
Over hearts that are hushed with a sudden surprise."

It is true that he took to occasional rhymes
With an art that was rather instinctive at times:
You might call it a genius; but what, in the test,
Is a genius for doing, but doing it best?

And although at poetic expression he caught
Half the grace of a poet, and added the thought
And the sentiment often, and many could praise
With a flattery honest his lyrics and lays,
He was not at his best in this work of his pen ;
For his speech was a power to move upon men :
And he held that the work of his life was to speak
As he might for the right, be it humble and weak ;
And his words were unfaltering, fearless, and strong
In the ears of the world in complaint of the wrong.
He was better at prose than at verse ; for he made
Every sentence to cut like the stroke of a blade
Never dull : he was quick to discover the sense
Of all sophistries subtle ; and every pretence
He would riddle and scathe with an irony born
Of his genuine honor, his marvellous scorn.

They had faith in his future, who frequently heard
His defence of the true ringing out till it stirred
Every heart to keen sympathy. But, as for him,
It was little he thought of the years that were dim
In the distance ahead. He was living to-day
With its needs and its gifts ; and no cynic could
    say
He was laggard of life. Full abreast of the hour
Did he keep, never sparing of work or of power.
He was spendthrift of being, without any heed
For the want of the morrow, its duty or need.

"Let the future take care of itself," was his thought:
"If I care for the present, as every man ought,
Do the work of a man with the will of a man,
'Tis enough."
     So he made neither purpose nor plan
For the future: he held no ambitious desire
To mount up on his deed to a deed that was higher.
No ideal he worshipped, of work or reward.
As if he were a servant, and labor his lord,
He would do every task that before him was set
With his might, and the wages of work would forget
In the pleasure of work, never counting it vain
That he wearied his body, and wasted his brain,
Without recompense fit; since instinctive he knew
That the best compensation for service most true
Is but had in the serving; that wages are small,
Be they measureless even, if wages are all.

Yet he wondered sometimes, in a curious way,
How to-morrow would differ in work from to-day;
What its spirit would be; what its impulse and scope;
What its faith and its feeling, its heart and its hope:
And so wondering often, he stood, as it seemed,
At the door of a duty of which he had dreamed
In some dream of great doing, — a something so broad
That it reached from his hand to the hand of his God,
Taking in by its infinite measure and span
The upholding of truth, the uplifting of man,

In especial degree; but he shrank as with fear
From the possible future, unsought and too near.
He was conscious that on in the years he would find
More of life than might add to the peace of his mind;
Yet so vaguely he felt it, so faint did it seem,
That he counted his consciousness only a dream,
And gave heed to it rarely.
                            One evening he wrote
In such mood to the friend of his heart, — just a note,
When the veil of his vision half lifted to show
A few glimpses beyond: —
                        "That you love me, I know;
That I love you, my darling, you feel just as sure,
And that both of our loves to the end will endure.
But the end? I am here face to face with the dread
That in pathways unlooked for my feet must be led;
That your life and my own are to drift far apart
As the true from the false. There's a cry in my heart
Of regret and dismay; for you measure the sum
Of my wishes and wants, and your love has become
The one thing of my craving, — none other so sweet
And so strong and so helpful. None other could meet
Just the need of my soul as you meet it. I feel
That you feel this and know it; and I should conceal
Such a fancy as here I have named, but that you
Have a faith that is strong, and a heart that is true,
And will say I am morbid, and need but your kiss
To return me the hope and the cheer that I miss.

"I have told you before of the fancy I hold,
That my work is to be by some duty controlled
Which I may not discover till years have gone by;
And perhaps through some wilds of experience I
Must pass in to my clear field of labor. My way
Has been sunny and bright all along till to-day;
But I know, as I know that I live, that there are
Heights and depths in my nature transcending by far
All that yet I have measured. No gift is for nought,
Be it even to suffer; and sorrow unsought
May bear fruit that is sweet from the bitterest seed.
You will see where this logic must certainly lead:
Any gift is for ultimate use. We may wait
All unknowing, unheeding, capacity great
To enjoy or to suffer; dead levels of life
May reach onward before us; the wearying strife
Of the days may go on without increase or rest;
We may seem of but commonplace being possessed,
With its commonplace ends to be met: but in time
To some great height of gladness we sudden may
  climb,
Or go down to some valley of grief, where the dark
Never knows a sun's rising or song of a lark
Singing straight into heaven, or amid all the din
Of the every-day battle some peace may begin,
Like the silence of God in its regal content,
Till we learn what the lesson of yesterday meant.

"But forgive me, my darling, for hinting of tears
In the possible future. What comes with the years
We'll accept as we may, never dreaming of pain
In the present; believing God's morrows are gain,
Be they cloudy or bright, let them hold what they will.
We are wedded to life, if for good or for ill,
Or for better or worse; and its issues must be
As is best and is wisest for you and for me,
If to-day we are faithful and trustful and true.
And so love me, my darling, as I must love you."

II.

"SHALL we go and hear Trent to-night, Bell, at the
    Hall?"

Major Mellen was making his afternoon call
On the witty and beautiful Isabel Lee,
Whom so often in leisure he dropped in to see.
They were cousins, by kin or by common consent:
If the former, 'twas distant.
                    "You've heard about Trent?"

"He who wrote that sweet thing in the last magazine,
Which you read me one night, — 'In my Passion
    Serene'?"

"Yes, the same. We were friends, he and I, long ago,
As I told you, I think. He's a man you should know, —
Can talk poetry, prose, metaphysics, or sing
His own songs to you even, with pathos to bring
The quick tears to your cheek. He has sentiment strong,
As you'll see by and by, when you weep at his song;
But reform is his hobby: he'll go for the Right
With a capital R, in his lecture to-night;

And they say as a speaker his powers are rare —
I've not heard him in years. But, good coz, have a care!
He's engaged to a lovely brunette, with dark hair
And pink cheeks, like yourself: were her beauty but
    blonde,
You might win him away with the contrast."
                                         "Beyond
Any question he's safe, my dear major. The man
Who can sing of a passion serene, as he can,
Must have little of passion to stir. I'm afraid
That your paragon wouldn't just-suit me, — too staid
And too deep. His philosophy matches not mine;
For love isn't as water. You sip it like wine,
And grow giddy and wild with the tasting. His words,
As you read them, were sweet as the singing of birds;
But I like not his faith." And her finely cut face
Had a look that was puzzling. The very least trace
Of surprise had the major's.
                              "You do not suppose,"
He remarked, "that the rhyme of a verse-maker shows
His true feeling? You never would take him to task
For philosophy, sentiment, worn as a mask
To conceal what is under? A woman will veil
What she feels in expression each lover must fail
To unriddle; and poets are privileged, too,
As to much that they say, if not all that they do.
If a poet pretend to write out of his heart,
It is mainly pretence; and the very best art

That he has is in making men weep while he grieves
Over fiction he never one moment believes,
But they swallow as fact."
       She looked up at him then
With a smile that he read as a sort of amen.

"And so be it, what then?" he continued. "Why, this:
All the woes of a poet are idle; his bliss
Never blisters the paper he pours out his life on;
His pen's not a patent, particular siphon
To run off the liquid of love, in his verse,
From his soul. If ecstatic, he's simply unreal:
His sonnets of love are to something ideal,
As the love that he sings."
      "You are bitter, now, major;
Sarcastic and bitter and foolish. I'll wager
You once took to sonnets yourself, when more callow.
Don't let any talent you've buried lie fallow;
Turn poet again, since the trick of deceit
You have learned (if the sum of all poetry sweet
Be pretence), which a poet must practise, and cover
Your faith and your feeling when you are a lover."

She laughed, — just a ripple of music from lips
That too often put pearly white teeth in eclipse;
And he echoed her mirth rather languidly.
        "Well,
It is certain I never plied you, Madame Bell,

With my sonnets," he parried; " and no other glances
Than yours could allure me to making advances
Afoot or on Pegasus *then*. I'll not say
By the light of whose look and whose smile I might stray
From my loyalty now. I confess I am grown
Rather fickle to love and to truth, as is known
To the most of my friends."
       And a smile half-sarcastic
Ran over his features so mobile and plastic.
" But this fellow Trent, he's as true, on my soul,
As the needle, much boasted, is true to the pole ;
Not but that a bright woman like you, cousin dear,
With an iron heart in her, if coming too near,
Might attract him and win him, and hold him a while ;
But he'd turn by and by from her lessening smile
To his star in the north."
      " To his passion serene,
He would say, I suppose. That remains to be seen " —

" And be tested? Perhaps. You must hear him to-night,
And then let me present him. His theme may be trite ;
But he'll say what he says in so pleasing a diction,
You'll think to be fact, philosophical fiction
The blankest, — at least for a little. No doubt,
When the ring of his words into silence dies out,
You will question your faith, and will count it absurd,
And be freed from it quite. But the song of a bird

You believe when you hear it (though haply it sing
Of some hope whose fruition no morrow may bring)
For the music that's in it; and Trent has a voice
That may even your sensitive hearing rejoice.
You will go if I call for you early?"

       "I'm free
To confess I would like this young poet to see,
Since you paint him so warmly. Invite him to sup
With us after the lecture. I'll brew him a cup
Of sweet compliments, if he deserve it, and learn
What he thirsts for the most from the world in return
For his gifts to the world, — whether praises or pence;
Whether garlands of roses, or blossoms of sense;
Whether wooing or worship. Your geniuses crave
Very much of their friends: you must serve them as slave,
Or cajole them as equal, with flattery sweet
To their taste; you must fawningly lie at their feet,
Or devotedly feed them with bonbons. The more
You bestow, will they ask. They're a terrible bore
To your patience, and make a most liberal drain
On your pity."

    "Be merciful, Bell! It is plain
That you're jealous of genius. Such comments as those
I must flatly resent." And he, laughing, arose.
"For we should not be blamed, who are pets of the stars
And the heirs of the gods. Any failing that mars
Our strict beauty of life is a fault half divine."
And with playful assumption, and graceful incline
Of the head in adieu, he departed.

                                    Her look
Of amusement departed as well, and she took
From the table a volume of verse that a friend
For her reading had lately been thoughtful to send, —
A collection of poems as varied in tone
As in merit.   But one of its pages alone,
As she absently turned them, arrested her thought, —
A few stanzas of sentiment, common, but fraught
With a passionate longing some time to be met
In the hope of the poet.   The name that was set
At the end caught her eye ere attention she lent
To the poem itself : it was *Percival Trent;*
And the title prefixed to the verse chanced to be
But suggestive of meaning.   It ran : —

BY THE SEA.

I stood one day beside the sounding sea,
   Amid a treeless waste of barren sand;
The billowy breezes soft blew over me,
   And wooed me sweetly with their kisses bland.

A subtle something lingered in their breath,
   And charmed me long to glad forgetfulness:
I thought no more of failure, pain, and death,
   No more I dreaded weakness and distress.

Far, far away the glistening billows gleamed,
   A-splendor with the summer's silver light;

And, looking seaward, blissfully I dreamed
    Of balmy islands somewhere out of sight.

And fondly still, with kisses warm and sweet,
    The breezes wooed me to a calm content;
While ocean, sounding softly at my feet,
    Its tuneful charm to the half-silence lent.

So with me ever, as I weary stand,
    And look far out upon the waters wide,
I catch some hint, in all the breezes bland,
    Of shady isles that somewhere yonder hide.

Where now I wait, a dreary waste may be,
    With no green thing to glad my longing eyes:
Far, far before, across the sounding sea,
    Are hid the balmy isles of Paradise.

As she read, her quick soul caught the cry of unrest
Welling up through the words, from a hungering breast,
And went answering out: for she stood, as it seemed,
By a waste of wild water whose billows ne'er gleamed
With the light of a sail bringing gladness and peace;
And she longed, with a longing that never might cease
Till she neared their glad haven of infinite calm
And content, for the Paradise Islands of Balm.
Could it be that across the wide deep, and beyond
All its possible shipwreck, there waited the fond
Wooing breezes of faith and of love? Would they seem
To her ever as more than a vanishing dream?

GERALDINE.

Would she find in their lingering kisses a quiet
From doubt and distrust that forever ran riot
Within her? Would hunger of heart, and the pain
Of unsatisfied want, and the wearisome reign
Of regret, have an end?
      So she questioned, and read
Yet again and again the brief stanzas that led
To a vision of loneliness dreary: —
         A man
Standing there by the sea where the sand-reaches ran
To slip under its waves and be hidden from view;
Far before him the shimmering billows of blue
Blending on with the tint of the sky; not a sail
In the distance to hint of a cheer-giving hail;
Not a bird flying over, with glint of its wings
To recall the sweet song that some dear singer sings;
And behind him no hills with their glories of green,
And a ribbon of silver soft winding between;
Only dull, level reaches of dry, barren sand
Sloping up from the sea, with no sign of the hand
Of a fellow in sight, not a house, nor a tree,
Only solitude, silence, and dreariness; he,
With his hungering eyes, looking out on the main,
With a longing of soul like the passionate pain
Of a lover unloved, — looking out to behold
Far away in the future, whose billows have rolled
Weary years at his feet, the fulfilment of life,
The incoming of love, like a peace after strife

Of long lasting, the ultimate gladness of time
Where the gladness and peace are forever sublime.

You may read all she read without seeing as much
As she saw: it may be that the delicate touch
Of her fancy is wanting; the mood that was hers
May not move you with sensitive impulse that stirs
To each breath of expression; no absolute need
May possess you, and hold you, till all that you read,
While you thrill in its holding, gives hint of reply
And revealing.   The fact matters not.

           By and by
She arose from her vision, came back to herself,
And the volume laid carelessly by on a shelf.
"It is idle," she thought, "to make pretence of woe
In this fashion.   No rhymes of a verse-maker show
His true feeling: the major was right." And she
  smiled.
"This new poet my sympathy quick has beguiled
Without any deserving.   It may be he missed
For a moment the touch of some lips he had kissed
Long ago; or it may be he felt but a blind,
Common craving for something beyond; or his mind
May have taken the most of its dolorous tone
From a liver disordered; or even my own
Vital organs may suffer,"—but, looking across
To the opposite mirror, she noted no loss

Of the color of health in her beautiful face,
And she laughed at the fanciful thought.
                              For the space
Of a half-hour she sat there alone in the room,
Till the shadows of twilight had gathered to gloom,
In a reverie deep. The rare smile faded out,
Giving place to a look as of questioning doubt;
And the eyes that had warmed many hearts with their
    glow
Had a tenderer light, as if tear-drops could flow
Without warning. Again she was living the past,
With no cloud of regret o'er its loveliness cast;
But just ready to bloom were her roses of youth:
She had faith in herself, she believed in the truth,
She could trust in her kind.
                              To be true to the best
That is in us, nor falter nor fail in the test,
Let whatever may come, — this is measurement just
Of the sum of our life; to keep safely in trust
All the good that we have, and to answer at length
For our being and doing, the weakness or strength
Of our hope and our help in the varying strife, —
There is nothing beside in this problem of life.

Had she faltered and failed in the test we have named?
If she had, by the perfect alone be she blamed.
It is easy to falter and stumble and fall;
But a pitiful God is the Father of all.

III.

"My Own Geraldine Hope, —

      "It is far in the night;
But I'm wakeful and restless, and so I will write
A few words for your reading before I retire.
I have had a long evening, yet short.

      "My desire
For an audience large and attentive was met;
I have never faced one more inspiriting yet.
When I rose to my feet, the same tremor possessed me,
The same idle terrors inthralled and oppressed me,
That often I feel in the face of a crowd;
But they vanished, so soon as I, trembling, had bowed,
And had uttered a word.

      "It is regal to stand
And to sway every will with a wave of your hand,
Or a shade of your voice. It is gladness supreme
To be thrilled for a time to the final extreme
Of your consciousness, through the quick thrill of your
   speech,
And to know of a certainty strong that you reach
And take hold of the hearts of your hearers; to feel
Their quick thrilling responsive; to know they are leal
To the kingship within you.

"The gift that is mine,
To a certain extent, is a dower divine,
And I shrink from its use, I confess, now and then.
It is such a grand mission, — to move upon men,
To determine their thought and their faith, to impel
Them to action, to guide and direct them, to tell
Where they miss the true path, where the pitfalls may
    wait,
To beget stronger love for the right, stronger hate
For the wrong. And, however we work, at the best
It is little we do that is well; for the rest,
May we lightly be judged!
                      "I began to recite
The events of the evening. Pray pardon the flight
Of my pen in this manner.
                      "The lecture was long,
But was brief to my thinking. I found in the throng
Of intelligent faces a few like your own, —
Of the answering sort, that one seems to have known
A long time; that respond to whatever you say
In a hearty and very encouraging way;
That a speaker soon learns to pick out here and there,
And to give them, perhaps, an unduly large share
Of his special attention. He reads the effect
Of his argument in them; he comes to expect
For his favorite thoughts recognition from these
That the mass may not give: it would seem that he
    sees

Not the many who hear him, but only the few
Who respond.
    "By the side of a man whom I knew
Years ago was a face of this type (not a face
To be quickly forgotten when met), with a grace
As of sorrow outgrown, but remembered, — a glow
Of unconscious expression illuming it so
As almost to transfigure it often. It had
A half-hungering look in repose, as if sad
Were the soul underneath it. 'Tis needless to add
'Twas a woman's, — a wife's or a widow's you'd guess
Without reasoning why; not because there is less
Of the sweetness of girlhood within it, but more
Of the woman's completeness of beauty.
        "Before
I had finished my lecture, I half comprehended
The secret hid under the face, and befriended
The womanly need, that so eagerly cried
In a speechless appeal to be soul-satisfied,
In my thought. When the lecture had come to an end,
And the people were slowly departing, her friend
Major Mellen presented me to her.
        "I've mentioned
The major, perhaps? He's a clever-intentioned,
Uncertain, erratic, and cynical man,
Who will ridicule always whatever he can;
Who is recreant, either in word or in fact,
To all truth; who can never make up what he lacked

As a boy, when I knew him at first, — a true sense
Of respect for things holy; who sees a pretence
In all earnestness, looks for deceit or a lie
In all candor, and laughs, with a tear in his eye,
At all sentiment sober; a man whom I shrink
From at times, yet who often compels me to think
That I like him, so shrewd are his comments, so keen
Is the wit that he flashes. I never have seen
Any human enigma more puzzling than he,
And I'm glad you don't know him, my dear.
                                    "Mrs. Lee
Is a woman of wit and of rare repartee,
With a lightness of speech that quite often belies
The suggestion of sorrow that lurks in her eyes.
They insisted that I should go with them to supper,
(She lives, let me say, in the style of the Upper
Ten Thousand, who dine very late, and sit down
To their tea at a time when the rest of the town
Is asleep :) I accepted, in hopes that a walk
In the chilly night air, and the major's bright talk
For an hour afterward, would beguile me to sleep.
And the major was witty and droll, if not deep,
Making odd little turns of the points of my speech,
And applying them oddly and keenly, till each
Of us laughed to the echo.
                        "The widow laughs well,
(She's a widow, I know, though I couldn't quite tell
How I know it;) has read the best authors in prose

And in poetry, current and classic, and knows
When to quote them and how, which is rather uncommon,
I'm tempted to say, nowadays, in a woman.

"A right merry season we had at the table:
I know 'twould amuse you in turn, were I able
To write out the many bright things that were said.
But all wit loses sparkle and glow when it's read,
And I'm not very good, I confess, at repeating
The many *bon mots* that I hear at a meeting
Like this, of a few who have sharpened their wits
By long practice. "I fancy the god of mirth sits
With his soul in the shadow, just ready to weep;
For so many I know, who in company keep
The whole roomful a-roar, are yet closest akin
To the pathos of being, and oft enter in
To the innermost temple of sorrow, where tears
Never gather and fall, and no grief of the years
Ever voices itself to the world. The great woe
Of a life (or I sometimes have reasoned it so)
May not be a great loss that it ever has known,
But a very great want that has silently grown
From an undefined need to the mastering strength
Of a hunger unfed, and that sways one at length
With an absolute will, — not a grief to be told
To a friend with a sigh, but to have and to hold
All unshared to the end.

"But enough of my fancies.
You'll come to believe that a hidden romance is
Beneath this new face I have met, if suggestion
Of sorrow be followed up thus. Beyond question
The woman has suffered, — a quite common case,
Very likely, though hers *is* an uncommon face;
And it may be her life has known nothing of lack
But in losing. I've promised to call, going back
From the West, and may more of her history learn.

"It is far in the night, and to sleep I must turn,
For my eyelids are heavy at last. May my dreams
Be of you and your love! Amid much that but seems
What it is not, I know that my darling is true
As the truth I believe and proclaim; and to you
The unrest of my heart ever turns for content:
So be tender and true to
                    "Your
                            "PERCIVAL TRENT."

IV.

So he called, as he promised, again and again;
And she met him with grace very charming. Few men
Ever failed to be won by the winning repose
Of her manner, to strong admiration. The close
Of each call came too soon. He would gladly have
    staid
Even longer, although it is true he delayed
His departure to etiquette's limits extreme.
He had met many women; had thought one supreme
O'er them all for her beauty, her sweetness, and grace:
But a charm quite elusive shone out of this face
That so puzzled his reading; a winsomeness new
In its every expression his interest drew;
And the touch of her hand as she bade him adieu
Was magnetic. Their talk was of places and books
At the first. He had been in some half-hidden nooks
Of the world, and, describing their beauties, would
    glow
With their memories rare. 'Twas his fortune to know
Men and women who write what the rest of us read;
And a word about books would so easily lead

To some personal gossip, they finally fell
Into serious thought as to what the books tell
Of the life and the love of their authors.
        "I doubt
If woman or man ever wrote much without
Weaving in their own story," she said. "I believe
In reality rather than fiction. Deceive
As some may the great public, who readily yield
To fictitious profession, there must be concealed
In each novel or poem that touches the heart,
And takes hold of the sympathies strongest, a part
Of the writer's own being and doing."
        "I hold
To another opinion. The poet is bold
In his fancy; the novelist free in the flight
Of imaginings many," he answered with quite
An emphatic expression, yet speaking as one
Who was weighing his words. "And, when you have
  begun
To determine where poet and novelist blend
With the persons they picture, there's never an end
To the questions arising; for either may be
As prolific in different pictures as he
Who is painting the crowd as they come. So diverse
Are the characters shown, that it couldn't be worse —
As a failure, I mean — if the painter should try
To be each of the persons he's painted. And why
Should we single out one of the many portrayed,

And declare that this one of the many is ma
Of the poet's own life, or the novelist's?"

"Now
You have taken to argument, I must allow
That my view appears weak," she returned with a
  laugh.
"But a woman ought never to argue; for half
That she knows is beyond demonstration. She feels
It to be, and so knows it to be; and conceals
Or confesses her meagre resources for knowing,
As moved by her whim. Yet there may be a show-
  ing
Of reason in what I have felt to be so.
Out of nothing no thing has been made, as we know,
That is good. Can a poet produce out of nought
What is living and real?"

     She paused.

       "But his thought
Is a something," he said, "and from this he produces
The beings that live and that love. In the uses
Of forms he is led to make copy of men
And of women he sees round about him; but, when
He puts soul into these, it is never the soul
Of another, not even his own."

      "Then the whole
Of his work is from fancy alone? If he write
With a heartache that throbs into words, 'tis the flight
Of his fancy-led thought, not a passionate cry

Out of sorrow he feels? And the many who sigh
As they read him are wasteful of sympathy?"
                                            Less
Of doubt did her words than her manner express,
And he felt that she studied him, striving to learn
Rather more than his answers might yield, in return
For her questions.
                  "Perhaps I should hardly declare
What you say to be true altogether. A share
Of the woe of the world may creep into its verse
Or its prose; but I doubt if a man will rehearse
Any grief of his own while a grief it remains.
He may journey beyond it, may think of its pains
As a thing of the past, and may write of it then
With a sort of contempt for its sacredness. When
It is part of to-day, he will shut it away
From the gaze of the crowd. I admit that he may
Seem to write of what is in the present, that urges
The blood in his heart to impetuous surges:
The heart may be throbbing, perchance, while he writes
What your sympathy moves, your emotion excites,
But from sympathy just like your own. He may feel,
When he writes with a heartache he does not conceal,
To the full the deep sorrow he breathes; but be sure
'Tis a grief that is fleeting, that will not endure,
That is born of his fancy, — the same as your own
While you read. And why not? Is the reader alone
To be moved by the syllables tender, the sobs

Welling up? I am certain the writer's heart throbs
Over sorrows of fancy as if they were true
And intense as the bitterest life ever knew."

"And how, then, may it be with his longings? Are
these
But the sigh of a moment, the breath of a breeze
Of desire blowing over him? Nothing he holds
Until it into beauty of being unfolds,
And makes glad some great need of his heart?"

Then he smiled.
     "Are you striving with logical art
Thus to prove me all wrong? It is in my beliefs
That the sorrow of sorrows, the grief of all griefs,
Is the sorrow, the grief, of a mastering need.
Yet a poet may syllable this; and indeed
I've no doubt that the longings of poets are real
As things that they long for are vague and ideal.
'Tis here that they reach after beauty and light
Far beyond and above all that gladdens their sight
In the present; and thus they uplift the whole race
With their longing and hoping and striving."
         His face
Growing earnest, she waited expectant.
        "To long
For some good that we have not is noble. The song
That incites to proud doing was penned with some hill

Of endeavor uprising before; and the will
To win glory and crowning sprang out of desire:
They only grow helpful and strong who aspire.
There is only one road to the mountains of bliss,
And it leads from the levels of longing."
                                        " But this
Is a general view you are taking," she said,
Interrupting him here with a smile. " I have read
Of some longings more special: their voice, like a call
From a hungering soul, on my heart seemed to fall,
And to wake a response. It was want crying out
To the plenty of life to be filled."
                                    " Beyond doubt
You have heard such a cry. Every soul not ascetic
Does hear it. The want of the world, so pathetic,
So broad, comprehends and embraces all needs,
Individual, hidden, and silent. The greeds
Of the world are past naming; the hunger and thirst
By which men are so often and sorely accursed
Are as legion: yet some one shall cry of his lack,
And at once the sad voices come echoing back,
As if truly this one had thus spoken for each,
When he wants something, maybe, that hangs within reach
Of the rest, and they think it is nought."
                                        " But there may
Be a want that is common to many. The sway
Of one mastering need, as you term it, may be
As supreme within you as it is within me:

It may hold just as firmly all sensitive souls.
We walk different paths; but the very same goals
Are to gladden us all by and by."

"But no twain
Are exactly alike in their longing. The pain
Of a wearing unrest in each heart is a thing
By itself, as by self to be borne. One may sing
A glad pæan of praise that the many outring
In re-echoing notes; but the song they are ringing
Had something his own, while his gladness was singing,
It lacks from the lips of another.

"I stand
By the oneness of each in himself. As the hand
That I hold to the world is my own, though it bear
A good gift of which all may claim portion and share;
So the poet may bring of his riches to such
As are needy, and each may be richer by much,
In the taking of what was his right, as it seems,
Out of common bestowal. But longings and dreams
That embody the gift are the poet's alone:
They are harvest, perhaps, of some seed he has sown
In the past. And no life may be like his so near
As to garner the same from its sowing."

"I fear
You are thinking too broadly to touch the one thought
I have had, and to answer it now. I have sought
To be sure of too much," she replied. "Let it go
Till I've pondered it further. You certainly know

Of my right as a woman to have the last word.
What you say may be true : if it be, I have erred
In conceding to poets the commoner woes
That afflict and make sad. I am bound to suppose
That you know of the facts." And he saw she had tired
Of their soberer talk, and so simply desired
By her badinage mild to glide off from the theme.

He but laughed, and made merry.
      "To-night, if I dream
Of some hunger of heart," he remarked, as he said
His adieu, "I shall know an invisible thread
From the heart of another my hungering thrills ;
That my want is the twin of your own ; that our wills
Are akin, and our needs?"
      He was reading her eyes
As he, bantering, questioned her thus for replies
That her tongue might not syllable. Nothing outshone
From their depths that gave answer complete.
      "I have known
What it is to be hungry of soul," she replied,
Speaking gravely again : "so have you, and, beside
Us, a host of the men and the women who greet
The gay world with a smile. It is easy to cheat
The blind mass into thinking we're glad and content.
It is hard to walk on with what fate may have sent
For your company, — hunger and doubt and unrest, —
And yet keep the heart steady that beats in your breast ;

It is hard to feel lonesome for love that is kind
To the uttermost, tender and trustful, and blind
To your ugliness, quick to discover your need,
And a spendthrift in giving itself."
        "May I plead
For one boon?" said he eagerly: "this, — be my friend,
As I'd like to be yours. Let me make some amend,
If I may, for the lack that you feel now and then,
And regret. I'll be frank : there is much that some men
Could bestow that I have not; the all I can give
Is but little, — a friendship that pledges to live
While you care for it, sympathy certain and strong,
And perchance here and there the glad note of a song
In your life as you find the way weary and sore.
I would give nothing less : I can give nothing more."

"It is much," she responded, "far more than you think.
When a wayfarer thirsty is given to drink
From a brook where the many may come and be filled,
He is glad as if never another were thrilled
By its current of blessing."
       She held out her hand,
And the pressure he gave it returned.
         "Understand,
We are friends while you wish it. Good-night."
          For what came
In the track of all this, they were hardly to blame.
There's a logic in life that is stubborn as fate :
We must learn it, each one, though our study be late.

V.

That Geraldine Hope was indeed a coquette,
Not a few were persuaded who met her, and yet
Without reason sufficient. Her smile, it is true,
Was bewitching, and freely bestowed. Then she knew
How to charm in those delicate ways that suggest
A particular feeling of interest. Pressed
For some cause for their thought as concerning her, these
Who esteemed her the least were at fault. By degrees,
As they knew her the better, they came to see under
The manner so winning at times, and to wonder
At womanly graces disclosed, at the will
To be helpful and brave; and they wondered until
They were champions strong of her truth.
        She had been
Greatly flattered and praised; and to please, and to win
Admiration, was easy. She studied no arts,
But was just her own natural self. If the hearts
Of men yielded her homage unsought, none could say
That she won it to scorn, or that he was the prey
Of deceit and delusion. No lover was pained
By the loss of a love that he never had gained
But in idle profession.

       The woman's soul in her
Was noble and true. To be won, he must win her
With truth and nobility equal, who brought
Her his heart and his life, and her heart and life sought.
And, beside, she must feel that he stood just above
Her in being and doing, whose life and whose love
Could be worthful and sweet, and in nothing below.
So she waited in faith, not unwilling to go
Through the years quite alone, if instead she must lean
On an arm that was lower.
       And thus Geraldine
By her suitors abundant had failed to be won,
Until Percival Trent, who had lately begun
To be known of the world, came to know her, and hold
Her supreme among women. His loving controlled
Her as never another's had done. He was king
Among men, in her sight, from the first; and the ring
That he gave her at last she would wear to the end,
Never doubting.
     If love could forever but lend
To its object the glow of perfection, how sure
Would all pledges of constancy be to endure!
"Love is blind," men have said; but they gravely
   mistake
Who believe so. Alas that it is not! The ache
That is born of regret would not vex and make sad,
If true love could not see; and a world would be glad
If no loving looked through the too common disguise

Of the thing winning love, and with grief-welling eyes
Saw the faults that lie under. We sorrow to find
That our friends are unworthy; and love is unkind
For revealing the fact, with its vision so clear,
That each life has its blemishes. Love may appear
As unseeing as marble, yet quiver with pain
From beholding so much; and the bitterest bane
Of the years will be found, as we learn what they teach,
In the knowledge that love gave a glamour to each;
That the beauty we saw could not always abide,
Nor the veil of our faith all deformity hide.

Had she trusted too much in this man who so held
All her life in his hand? who so surely compelled
Her to trust him and love him? Not hers was the
    question:
No doubt troubled her, nor the faintest suggestion
Of doubt. He was hers; she was his. Before God
They were wedded forever. Their way might be broad
In the future, or narrow: it could not prevent
Them from walking together in happy content
To the gate that leads out of this being. Beyond
There should dawn an eternity, never less fond
In its faith and its love; and the bliss of her dream
Should be endless at last where all love is supreme.

So she thought. To his questioning letter she made
An unquestioning answer: —

"Dear heart, I'm afraid
You are working too hard, and need rest. By and by
You will smile at the dread you have named, as do I.
There is nothing to fear in a love that is strong
And content as is ours. If the time should be long
Ere I see you again, I should never once doubt;
If long years should roll by us uncertain, without
Bringing word of remembrance from you, I should know
There were reason for silence, and patiently go
Up and down at my duties, in trust. If a living,
Abiding affection is formed, the up-giving
Is perfect, of life and of faith : there can be
Neither question nor fear. As for you and for me,
We rely on a love that is higher by much
Than our own to mould ours, and to keep it. The touch
Of this love so divine adds a quality rare
To our own ; makes it pure beyond any compare
With the commoner loves ; makes it lasting and sweet
And immortal.

"I think there can be no defeat
For a love that is guarded by trust. It withstands
Every effort of cruel and violent hands
To dethrone it; it rules with a wonderful might,
Born of weakness and yielding ; it strives for no right
But the right to bestow of its largess ; it speaks
With an eloquent tongue, in a silence that seeks
But to hear the dear words of bestowal ; it waits
For the gladness of time that its faith antedates,

And is glad in its waiting; it patiently bears
Every strain of the years, all the grief and the cares
They may bring; it is faithful and true to the end:
And we know such a love, I am certain, my friend.

"As for duty, that's God speaking plainly to each
Of his work in the world; and the wider the reach
Of your effort, the more you are doing for men,
Then the sweeter will be your reward. So what, then,
Does it matter concerning a duty to come?
Every morrow grows out of to-day; and the sum
Of the future is made from the present. Whatever
The morrow may bring will depend on endeavor
Put forth by us now. If to-day we are strong
In the right, need we fear that a possible wrong
In the future will find us unwilling and weak?

"Let the way that we journey be rugged and bleak
By and by: we may smile as we wander to-day
Where the roses are blowing, and fancy the way
Is forever to lead amid beauty and bloom.
If we know that the sunshine will vanish in gloom,
Let's be glad till the shadows are on us.

"No man
And no woman of right should the coming days scan
With foreboding. The present is ours; and the rest—
That is God's. He will care for his own as is best;
And our watching is worthless, our dread is in vain.

Are we moulded to suffer? The possible pain
Will not easier seem for expecting it. Waits
Any wretchedness for us? The hardest of fates
May be sweetened by love and a song of good cheer,
Like a psalm in the night.
      "There is nothing so clear
To me ever, dear heart, as that strength will be lent,
If we ask it, to bear what the Lord shall have sent;
And that every hard duty will find us with strength
To attempt, and indeed overcome it, at length,
If we cling to the Giver of strength, nor let go
When the weakest we feel. For I'm certain, I *know*,
That the weakest may hold to God's hand with a grip
That is ever unyielding, if only the lip
Can say, 'Help me, O Father!' so quickly he hears,
And so soon is he touched by our need and our tears."

Such a faith is a treasure of blessing: it yields
The sweet waters of peace in the barrenest fields.
She will need all the help that it offers to cope
With the want of her morrow — poor Geraldine Hope!

VI.

Major Mellen had business in Rivermet; leisure,
When business was done, to bethink him of pleasure.
He called upon Geraldine Hope, —
                             "Just to show
That I have not forgotten that summer, you know,
When we met at the Hills," he remarked.
                                  With a trifle
Of speech she replied, as if willing to stifle
His thought of the past.
                      "It is ages since then,"
He resumed. "I have waited for fate once again
To be kind, but in vain — until now."
                                   "You believe,
Then, in fate?" she abruptly inquired.
                                    "Yes, I grieve
To admit that I do," was the answer, a touch
Of distrust in his manner; "that is, quite as much
As I'm apt to believe in things ever. They say
I'm a heretic born, and have wandered away
From all faith in the good and the true. It's a libel
Of course." And he laughed. "I've a beautiful Bible
I read every day — when the weather is fine.

(You may open your eyes at this statement of mine
In mute wonder.)   The book is as broad as the sky,
And as old as the world.   If a poet, I'd try
To repeat the sweet promises in it, to tell
What it says to me often, so wondrously well
That I listen enrapt; but I haven't the gift
Of expression.   There's Trent" —
       At this mention the swift-
Coursing blood from her heart, leaping into her cheek,
Told him more than all words that her loving might
  speak;
But he seemed not to heed the quick witness.
        " His tongue
Or his pen, for the sweetest of songs ever sung,
Could find words in my Bible, I'm certain.   The book
Is the richest I know; and who wishes can look
At it even as I do, with longing to learn
All its lessons and secrets.   I turn and return
To its pages each summer with pleasure intense."

They were often beset with perplexing suspense
Of his meaning and purpose, who listened to him;
And she heard him run on, with a consciousness dim
That he might have a motive in speaking, not quite
To be seen at the outset.
      " That week of delight
In the mountains, when fate was so winningly kind
As to show me your face, I was never less blind

To the beauties the great book of Nature revealed,
And I revelled in loveliness. Forest and field
Had a charm for me new. Every mountain-top shone
With a marvellous glory. I think, had I known
'Twas the very last week of my life, I'd have cared
Not at all. I am seldom ecstatic; I've fared
At the best and the poorest so often, I hold
By philosophy cool, as a rule; but the gold
Of that summer week's gilding is bright even yet:
I must live through a lingering age to forget
All the glamour and glow of those days that went past
Like a dream of content."
      " Was that summer the last
That you saw of the Hills?"
        She was puzzled to tell
What to think of his words and his manner. So well
She remembered his cynical smile and his sneer,
Half-disguised, at all sentiment tender, and dear
To the sensitive heart, she could hardly accept
What he uttered as earnest.
       " I could not have kept
My first love for the Hills,—for those Hills,—had I
  been
There again. The one visit was all. It's a sin
To defraud any pleasure, of sight or of deed,
By repeating it. One of the rules that I heed
Is to go only once to a place, if I go
For mere pleasure alone; and, remembering so

But the freshness and zest of my pleasure most keen,
There is nothing to me that is common, I mean,
In the matter of scenic delight."

"You forget
That last evening we waited to see the sun set
On the top of Mount Vision," she said in reply.
"You were silent a while; but the glow of the sky
Was reflected, I thought, in the glow of your face.
You had seen the same picture; the very same grace
Of superlative beauty in color and tone
Had beguiled you again and again "—

"But it shone
In a different light; it was not the same view;
It had different tints, and a different hue
Over all from the sunsets we commonly see.
And, moreover, two sunsets are never to me
Just alike. They are even diverse as the features
Of men in expression. The creeds of the preachers
Can vary no more. But your lakes and your hills,
Your meadows and mountains, your rivers and rills,
Are the same to the end of the chapter: they yield
Nothing fresh for renewed admiration; revealed
Is the sum of their beauty at first to your eyes:
They are changeless, in short. But the sea and the
    skies,—
These are changeful as man, and, because of their
    change,
As bewitching as woman."

"Such talk would seem strange
From another than you, Major Mellen, indeed.
I am puzzled by logic that lightly can lead
To conclusion like yours. You would find your delight
In the face of a stranger; and even the sight
Of a friend would be wearisome, just in degree
As the friend were familiar to you."

"It might be
As you say," he responded, "if 'twere not the fact,
As I've hinted, that faces do change; and an act,
Or a thought, or a hope, or a feeling, may bring
A new face in the old. But your bird there may sing
A new song, though he change not a feather; and thus
May our friend, though he change not the smile he
    gives us,
Be as changeful in words as the sky is in looks,
Have as varying moods as the sea, or the books
Of the poets."

"Perhaps" (and she paused, as if shrinking
From saying too much) — "it may be we are thinking
Diversely. I never am positive whether
Your words and your thoughts run exactly together.
You like to combat and discuss, and draw out
The beliefs and the fancies of others. I doubt
If you fully accept all you freely imply.
Now, to me every mountain takes glow from the sky
That it kisses, or sombreness wears like a frown
When the mists and the shadows fall heavily down;

Every meadow lights up by the sun, as a face
Might be glorified, seen in some radiant place;
Every lake but reflects what the sky above shows, —
Either sunlight or shadow; it sparkles and glows,
Or is angry from touch of the winds, or is still
As the spring that begets yonder musical rill
In its home in the wild. I see changes in all
That are beautiful. None of these ever can pall
On my vision."

    He often had seen her as now,
With the pink of her cheek and the white of her brow
Yet the stronger in contrast, from feeling that urged
The quick blood through her veins till it rippled and
  surged
In her face. He had often beguiled her to think
In expression as earnest, that thus he might drink
Of her glowing delight in the lovely and true:
'Twas a pleasure surprising, peculiar, and new,
Thus to put her in eager defence of her thought,
Till her beauty, with something mysterious fraught,
Had a charm that was rare. He had wearied of much
That men fancy is pleasant; but here was a touch
Of delight that he could not explain. He could smile
At the commoner pleasures with which men beguile
The dull days. But some influence hidden, unguessed,
Was upon him, and gave to each moment a zest
That was fresh and unfailing, as, scanning her face,
He could study her feeling and thought, and could trace

Every turn of her fancy, each questioning doubt.
He had keen intuition, and saw much without
Any effort at seeing; was quick to divine
Every meaning that lurked in a glance or a sign;
And made use of his sceptical questions and sneers
To uncover the souls of his friends.
      "It appears
To me certain *you've* read in my Bible," he said,
With a laugh not too mocking, "although you have read
With a thought of your own running on with the theme
Of the text. *You* can linger and listen and dream
In the woods and the fields like a poet, — or, yes,
Like a man of the world who forever finds less
In the world to his fancy, except it be far
From the din — and the dinners. You certainly are
Of the order of poets yourself, to behold
Such a glow of the new in a shade of the old.
You should marry a poet, Miss Hope, who could see
With such eyes as your own — if there happen to be
Any man of so wealthy endowment."
        She blushed
At the words and the look, and unconsciously crushed
A wild rose she had held in her hand. Had he heard
What one poet was to her?
      "It never occurred
To me, major," she said, "that the ultimate mission
A poet may know is to bring the fruition
Of life to one woman he honors with marriage.

I may not be right, — and I would not disparage
The poets, I'm certain, — but poets, as poets,
Belong, I believe, to all women. I know it's
A fact that they marry; but isn't it fact
That they wed not as poets? that women attract
Not the poet, but only a man among men?"

He was puzzled, in turn, for a moment, and then,
Comprehending that she was but parrying, laughed,
And let fly, as he fancied, a Parthian shaft.

"No, they *don't* wed as poets : connubial ties
Would be idle to bind all the passion that lies
In the heart of a poet. The man may be bound;
But the poet is free, and wherever is found
Any blossoming sweet he may gather it in.
They are lucky — these poets : they've only to win
As the men, like us all, and have freedom accorded
To woo and to win, then, as poets, rewarded
By beauty and love in most bountiful measure.
A poet, it seems, has an infinite leisure
For love, and capacity equal. There's Trent,
Whom I've named : the good fellow was meant
For a knight in heroic and chivalrous times
Quite as much as a minstrel to maunder his rhymes.
He's the soul of a poet, as all will confess
Who have heard him and read him; likewise (and not
  less)

Is the liberal heart of the poet his own.
We were intimate friends years ago; but I've known
Very little about him since then, till of late.
As a boy in his teens, he'd a singular fate
For sporadic affection: before he was twenty
He'd loves half a dozen; it's probable plenty
Have gladdened him since. It was thought he would
    wed
A young lady in Somers; and I have heard said
He would marry some one in this town."
                                    "Did you hear
Who the young lady was?" she inquired with a queer
Little tremor of voice.
                      "Now I really forgot
To inquire," he replied; "but the fact matters not.
He's a passion much later than that, I am sure,
And it may prove more difficult even to cure.
I have known more than one to meet Isabel Lee
To his lasting regret. She's a marvel to me
(And a cousin, which means that I know her quite well)
For her mastery over the men. I could tell,
When I introduced Trent, what would follow. She
    knew
How to rouse his whole interest in her. She drew
Him again and again, and will draw him, despite
Any previous fancy, until her delight
In his presence and passion is over. The hurt
Will not kill him."

"This woman is, then, but — a — flirt,"
She remarked, hesitating, to cover the pause
When he stopped.
"I may say she has given some cause
To be called so," he answered, a cynical ring
In his voice; "but she may not intend any thing
That is certain to breed very positive harm.
She believes in the right of each woman to charm
As she can. She regards it the duty of each
To do discipline-work on all hearts within reach.
She's a woman of women, in short, with a will
To be wooed for the wooing, not won; to instil
As much love as she may in the hearts of mankind,
Which is quite evangelical truly. We find
That the preachers preach love, of a sort; and the best
Should be fruiting itself in humanity's breast,
If occasion there be for the poorest."
He talked
In a tone that was usual with him, and mocked
All the meaning his cynical words might have held;
And she listened with curious feelings, compelled
To seem anxious as only a woman who heard
Such allusion to one of her sex as but stirred
Her own pity indignant. Her face was aflame,
And she dared not to venture on speaking his name
Who was more to her even than life.
"It's a shame,"
She made answer, "for women to be as you say.

And you libel us all when you speak in that way,
As if women were all mere coquettes. There are more
Who give love than are loved; and, if all men but bore
The respect that they ought for all women, the sex
Would be nobler and better. You talk but to vex
Me to earnest defence of my kind: you don't mean
What you utter."
     He smiled, the same smile she had seen
On his face in the past, — half a sneer, half assent
To a fact he would gladly refute.
         " I'm content
Not to argue the question," he answered, " with one
Who might point to herself, ere we well had begun,
As a proof for all women. I gladly cry quits
At the outset. I never could measure my wits
With a woman's in argument. Even to try,
In this instance, would lose me my train: so good-by."
And he rose, and extended his hand.
         " Must you go?"
She replied; not too eager, he fancied. " I know
The young woman — you heard about — here, whom
  your friend
Was to marry," she went on to say, " and will lend
Her my ears for the news you have brought, should it
  seem
To be worth any while."
       And like one in a dream
She went up to her room, and sat down with her grief

Over-brooding and weighing upon her.   Belief
In the story to which she had listened was first
A necessity.   All it implied, and the worst,
She accepted, and tortured herself into pain
Of the keenest.   When day came again, she had lain
On a bed of unrest a long night through ; her throbbing
Heart weary and tempted, and sore with its sobbing ;
For the woman within her was quick to take up
Any bitterness offered, and drink till the cup
Had been drained to its dregs.
       Then some gladness shone in :
She was wicked to yield to her doubt ; it was sin
Thus to sorrow and grieve ; if some love she had lost,
There was God, — he would profit her, even at cost
That was dear.   So she reasoned, at length ; and she
   prayed
With a tender upgiving that must have delayed
More than one of God's angels to listen and hear.
And at last, through the clouds, came a radiance clear,
Till she saw mid her tears the glad rainbow of trust.

When believing came back, — as to some hearts it
   must,
Though it leave for a little, — she felt she had done
A great wrong to her love and to God ; and, as one
Who has grievously sinned, she repented in tears
Of her sin, till they blinded her doubts and her fears,
And made way for the sunshine that came.

                                And how sweet
Is the sunlight that falls on our wandering feet,
When the morning dawns clear after night of distress,
And we look on a land that our hope may possess
By and by! Blessed morrow to gladden us all,
If to-day not a shadow of sunset could fall!

VII.

When Geraldine Hope met her lover again,
She was tenderer even than common. To men
Of his mould it is easy for women to yield
Their caresses and trust. She had always revealed
Her whole soul to him freely; and now she expressed
With sweet emphasis, sweeter than any possessed
In articulate language of love, how she rested
Herself in his heart. It was not that she tested
His love and his faith: she was certain of these;
She had walked from her wilderness dark on her knees.
It was not that she thought to make certain her strength
Over him, as of old; it might happen at length
That she seem to him weaker than late she had been
In the sight of herself. It was not that she win
A new fervor of love. It was simply that he
Had been wronged in her thought and belief; and so she
Made amends as she could.
     There are wives who have doubted
The faith of their husbands for less, and have shouted
Their doubts to the world, as if virtue must claim
Its reward on the house-tops, or ally with shame;
But this woman, as wedded by love, in the eyes

Of the angels, she knew, as her sister that sighs
Over vows, and a bridal ring empty of bliss,
Could seal close into silence her pain with a kiss,
And remember it only to smile at. She would not
So much as make question to him ; and she could not
Again feel a question concerning his love,
She was trustingly sure. And henceforth, far above
Every statement of cynical doubt, she would bear
Her belief in his honor and truth. He should share
The full trust that she gave to her God.

        You may know
How she loved, to stand fast and unfaltering so ;
You may guess what her love must have meant to her life,
When she fought out alone such a wearying strife
With distrust, and then put it all back in the past,
That no shadow of conscious unfaith might be cast
On their future.

      Had Percival Trent at this time
Felt a doubt of his love in return, some sublime
And unselfish intent must have moved him to hold
It in check. He was tenderer, too, than of old.
He looked down in her eyes with his own brimming over
With truth, and was glad.

        "I've so long been a rover,"
He said to her soon, "that I hunger for home
Of my own. Only vagabonds always can roam
Up and down, as a decade or more I have done,
Without wearying of it. There's much to be won

In the broad world of being I've studied so long;
But I'd rather be singing some ingleside song
For your heart to be happy in hearing alone,
Than to win all the praises of men I have known.
I've another long season of labor ahead,
That will amply provide me with means to buy bread
For us both afterward. You'll be ready to sit
And preside for us two at the breaking of it?"
She could be very merry indeed, if. she chose,
And the spirit was on her just now.
         " I suppose
We may have something more," she remarked with a
  laugh,
"Than you've mentioned? For me, I must say, even
  half
Of a loaf would not answer. A little of meat
And potatoes might make our provision complete."

"It is meet we shall be at our own little board
By and by," he rejoined, " when my slow-growing hoard
Is increased to the proper proportions. We'll live
On the peaches and cream of existence, and give
Of the commoner good to who wants it."
         She smiled
At his liberal purpose. She seemed like a child
In her simple acceptance of pleasures to be,
And she listened with joy that was winsome to see
As he glowingly pictured the happy content
Of some morrow to come.

Surely Percival Trent
Was a fortunate man. With his mood at its best,
He was glad as are they in the Valley of Rest
Who have never a sorrow, and never are sad;
He could stand on the Mountains of Beulah, as glad
As if never he groped in the shadows below,
And the glories of being as truly could know
On their heights as if down in the depth there were none
Of its midnight and gloom when the gladness was done.
Yes, a fortunate man, but more fortunate here,
On this day of delight, than in many a year,
If forever, he might be again; for he stood
On the edge of his Edom, unknowing. The good
Of the Uplands of Promise could only be gained
By a wilderness way that was rugged, and stained
With the blood of its wandering, wearying souls.
He must go as they journey who seek for the goals
That are hardest to gain, with no kindness or care
For himself, only patient, and willing to bear
All the pain of the days, all their famishing heat.
May God help him, if ever the manna sent sweet
From the generous heaven should fail in his need!
God help all who are seeking their Canaan, and lead
As he can, with his merciful hand of release,
By and by, to its infinite plenty and peace!

When they parted at last, Geraldine and her lover,
The angels of hope seemed to heed them, and hover

About them with whispers of cheer. It was June;
And the air, with its murmurous music in tune
With their sentiments tender, was sweet as a breeze
From some island of bloom, blowing over the seas
To a mariner homesick for land. 'Twas a time
To be wed, and not parted. The year in its prime
Was a redolent glory; the thrill of its bliss
Added ecstasy rare to the thrill of their kiss
As he said his farewell.

There are days that are kind
As a mother to men, showing pathways that wind
Out and in, like a dream, by some stream of delight;
Never hinting of aught that they hold to affright;
Only luring us on, since the way must be trod,
Over meadows of green with their velvety sod,
To the steeps, that are harder to climb, far before.
There are nights so enchanting, they seem to restore
The original beauty of Eden; so tender,
They woo every soul to a willing surrender
Of feverish longing; so holy, withal,
That a broad benediction seems sweetly to fall
On the world.

And these followed with magical sheen,
The rare sunsets aflame the rich mornings between,
Giving Percival Trent a new relish for life,
A new spirit and grace for the struggle and strife
Of the years. For he went for his summer's brief rest
Down a river of beauty to Isles of the Blest.

VIII.

Fair St. Lawrence! What poet has sung of its grace
As it sleeps in the sun, with its smile-dimpled face
Beaming up to the sky that it mirrors? What brush
Has e'er pictured the charm of the marvellous hush
Of its silence, or caught the warm glow of its tints
As the afternoon wanes, and the even-star glints
In its beautiful depths? and what pen shall betray
The sweet secrets that hide from man's vision away
In its solitudes wild? 'Tis the river of dreams.
You may float in your boat on the bloom-bordered
    streams,
Where its islands like emeralds matchless are set,
And forget that you live, and as quickly forget
That they die in that world you have left; for the
    calm
Of content is within you, the blessing of balm
Is upon you forever. Mortality sleeps
While you dream, an immortal: some mistiness creeps
Like a veil of forgetfulness over your past,
And it is not. Your day is eternal, to last
Without darkness, or change, or the shadow of dread.
Blessed isles where to-day and to-morrow are wed

In such fulness of bliss ! Blessed river that smiles
In such beauty and peace by the beautiful isles !

He had dreamed for a week at the Islands, content
Without company, glad of each lonely day spent,
And shunning the groups that each evening convened
At the house where he stopped. But one night, as he
        leaned
Looking out of his window, some fair sailors singing
Far over the water, their sweet echoes ringing
But faintly across the dim distance, he heard
A clear voice in the portico under, that stirred
Him to interest sudden and strong. Could it be
That he listened aright? He would walk down and see.
There was only one woman who had such a tone,
Among all the women he ever had known ;
Such a mellow out-gushing of melody clear
As made music of commonplace speech to the ear.
When he passed to the portico broad, there was none
To be seen whom he knew ; for the band had begun
Its accustomed performance within the great room
Where the gay ones had gathered: outside was the gloom
Of an evening whose moon was unrisen. The shout
Of some fishermen smote the soft air, and died out
Into silence. The song from the opposite shore
Had been sung to the end. The soft dip of an oar
In the water so still was the sum of all sound
From without. Disappointed, he went the whole round

Of the ample verandas, expectant, but met
No reward for his searching, and turned with regret
To the place where the dancers were waiting.
        A bright
Scene it was that he saw, — the large room all alight,
Happy groups here and there gayly chatting and laugh-
 ing,
Here and there a coquette her blind followers chaffing,
Some silent ones simply observing or dreaming,
The glitter of fashion and radiance gleaming
Throughout. It was strange he had willingly staid
From such music and glow as here met him. He
 made
His way quietly into the room, and sat down
To look over the faces, — some sun-burned and brown
From the water and wind, and a few that were tinted
With color so vivid and strong, that they hinted
Of rouge. There were none he had seen, save at table;
And out of the tumult, the blare, and the babel
The band and the people were making, he caught
Not the one single tone that his listening ear sought:
Yet he waited, and listened, and almost forgot
What he came for, and missed. 'Twas his fortunate lot
To like music so well, that it counted for much
That he wanted; at times making up, with its touch
As of magic, the lack and the need.
        By and by,
When the dancers were weary and still, with a sigh

He went out, and strolled down to the wharf, where the
    boats
Lay awaiting the morrow. Some late singer's notes
Came across to him there from the shadows beyond
The broad channel, and wooed him to dreams that were
    fond.
But just over the tree-tops the meek moon was hung,
Its soft lustre illuming the stream ; and he swung
A light skiff from its place, and laid grip on the oars.
He could handle them well. In a moment the shores
Faded out into dimness ; the mammoth hotel
Was a glittering spot in the night; and he fell
Into musing profound.
      From his boat far away
To the slow-sailing moon, on the waters there lay
A broad pathway of gold, for his fancy to take,
And go up to the region of dawn, and there make
A new morning ideal. The wash of the waves
On the boatsides was like the low-murmuring staves
Of a Mendelssohn's Song without Words, and inclined
Him to utter forgetfulness. Patient, and blind
To the sins of the world, the pale stars shone above him ;
The balmy night-breezes seemed shyly to love him,
And kiss him with clinging, affectionate grace ;
And unmindful of time, and unheeding of space,
He was borne down the current. Some strains of a song
Floated over him, echoing faintly along
On the silence ; but heard (if at all they were heard),

As you hear the loud carolling call of your bird,
Without heeding. His soul had companionless gone
To the realm of the silent, the land of the dawn.

So he mused and he dreamed; but a-sudden his dreams
Were all shattered and sunk by the shivering screams
Of a little steam-yacht that was running him down
In the stillness and dark.
      "He will certainly drown!"
Said a voice in affright, as the vessel's light bow,
Deftly cutting the deep, slid along on the prow
Of his boat, and upset it. Dismay seized on all
In the yacht, and a common and terrified call
Woke the echoes around.
      "Ship ahoy!" said the man
From his bath in the night. "Lend a line, if you can,
And I'll right up my boat, and make fast for a tow."

As he swam to his craft that had floated below,
He recalled the one voice that had spoken at first,
And was certain a friend must be near. At the worst,
He could count on a cold for his droll escapade:
There was nothing of danger.
      The yachtsmen obeyed
His request, flung a line, and bore round to him quick.

"Come on board!" said the captain. "A very poor
  trick

We have played you, whoever you are. Can't be mended
As *I* see, however: so don't be offended,
But give us your hand." And he lifted him up
To the rail all a-dripping. "A good brimming cup
Of my brandy will keep you from taking a chill.
Let me bring you a drink."

        "No, I thank you: I will,
If an overcoat be at command, accept that;
And, if some one had only the twin of my hat
That I left in the water, I think I might wear it."

"It hadn't a brick in to sink it, I'll swear it!"
Said one of those nearest, outreaching his hand.

"Is it *you*, Major Mellen? I quite understand
My disaster at once. Melancholy the place
And occurrence, indeed."

       "But you put a good face
On it, all must admit, Mr. Trent," said the voice
He had heard. "We must all of us keenly rejoice
That it ends no more sadly."

        "And *you*, Mrs. Lee?
To bring up in such circle, I'd e'en go to sea,
As the Wise Men set sail, in a bowl." And he took
The white hand that she offered him warmly. It shook
With the faintest of tremors.

        "Pray pardon me, each,
For the fright I have caused you. I might make a
  speech

To the party, without the least possible fear
Of (for once) being dry."
     " Then pray make it right here
And just now," said the major. " Don't let it go past.
Such a chance should be met, for it may be the last.
I present to you, ladies and gentlemen, one
Who appears on the scene like a genuine son
Of the sea, Mr. Percival Trent. You have read
Him in prose and in verse. It has often been said
That his measures are liquid, the reason is plain:
He inclines to the liquid himself."
        So the vein
Of good humor was worked till they landed, and said
Their good-nights, and betook them to silence and bed.

IX.

It was late the next morning when Percival Trent
Took his breakfast. At table a message was sent
To him, asking that he would make one of a number
To seek the Canadian channel. Sweet slumber
Had rendered but idle all fears of his friends
With regard to his health, as with humor that lends
A rare aid to digestion, he sauntered below
To the landing. The party was ready to go, —
A gay group whom he hardly had noted last night,
And for whom he cared little to-day. But the sight
Of his friend Mrs. Lee gave him pleasure afresh.

"Is it, then, really you whom I see in the flesh,"
She inquired with a smile, "and not simply your spirit,
That startled us there from the river?"

"I fear it
Was I in the flesh who so frightened you all,
As this certainly is; though I seem to recall
As a very vague dream my unpleasant relapse
Of last evening. I've met with more wretched mishaps,
But not often. The fault was my own, and the scare

You all kindly took part in. I'll use better care
The next time I go dreaming alone, Mrs. Lee."

"But pray tell, Mr. Trent, how you happened to be
Solitary and far, as you were, and so late.
I have never supposed you a tempter of fate
In such manner unsocial."
      "I'm here quite alone,"
He made answer. "No soul whom I ever have known
Have I seen for a week, till last night I met you
And the major. I like to be captain and crew
Now and then, and go drifting wherever the stream
May incline me. The moonlight invites me to dream,
And a dreamer is ever unsocial. But pray,
Are you here for the season, or only a day?"

"For a month, Mr. Trent; and I hope you will stay
While we tarry. My friends would not take a denial,
And brought me along *nolens volens*. My vial
Of wrath at their folly is empty at last;
For I think I could bear it a while to be cast
On a desert indeed, with both you and the major
To cheer me."
    "You're talking of me, I will wager,
In ways that you should not," that gentleman said,
Coming up. "But no matter, I've been for the bread
And the butter, and pickles, and now we are going
Aboard."

The small steamer her whistle was blowing
In little shrill screams that suggested his waking
From reverie deep the night previous. Taking
Their way to the yacht, they were off very soon
For a morning's delight, and a long afternoon
Mid the islands that skirt the Canadian shore.
It was one of those days to stand out evermore
In your memory, after you live them, divine
From the Maker's own hand, with a shimmer and
    shine,
And a marvellous glow that are rare as the mornings
Of God. And all Nature had donned the adornings
Of beauty, and wore them with grace like a queen.
Every islet seemed glad in its garments of green;
And the far-away hills of the mainland were beaming
With brightness against the blue sky.
                          Slowly steaming
Adown the wide channel for two or three miles,
They then rounded their course for the Lake of the
    Isles.
How it sleeps, with the islands embracing it round,
In its beautiful, silvery silence profound!
The sweet charm of content is upon it, unbroken
By sound of unrest, or the presence or token
Of man. There is nothing to trouble the dreams
That are born of its beauty, save haply the screams
Of some hawk as he greedily chases his prey,
Or the plash of a fish in the water.

"Some day
I would die in a beautiful silence like this,
And go out of the world with the world's tender kiss
Sweet upon me," said Trent, in a low underbreath,
To the friend at his side.
"Don't remind me of death
In the midst of such beauty and peace," she replied.
"I would live on forever within it!"
She sighed;
But her face wore a smile as she spoke.
"I'm a heathen
You'll think, Mr. Trent; but no fancy to me than
The fancy of death is more dreadful. I can't
Overcome it. It's foolish, I'm ready to grant;
But I shrink from all thought of just dying — just
    giving
Up breath, and so — stopping forever. My living
Don't count for so much, I admit, as it might,
For myself and my friends; and I value it light
As you possibly could do. It isn't that I
Am so anxious to live; but I don't want — to die."

They were sitting, it chanced, just a trifle apart,
And unheard by the rest.
"It is not in the art
Of the preacher to make such a commonplace thing
Of this dying as some would fain make it. The sting
Of mortality is and must be that it perishes.

Nothing can last that the heart fondly cherishes
Here "— and he paused.

"Yes, of course. And I know
That this body of mine, and this being, must go
Very soon the one way of all flesh; yet the thought
Is a horror to me — that our bodies are brought
Into life for a little, to trouble and care for,
To keep, and at times, perchance, put up a prayer for;
And loving them much, it may be, from such caring,
We then must accept for them only the faring
Of death and the grave. We were made, I believe,
For a destiny better."

"Some error of Eve
Played the mischief with destiny, I have been told,
If to answer your comment I may be so bold,"
Said the major, approaching, who heard the last sentence.
"The whim of a woman, the lasting repentance
Of man, — that's the way it has been ever since.
While the whims amuse you, they may cause us to wince
Pretty often. I'm 'posted,' — I carry the scars."
And he laughed as he spoke.

"But not one of them mars
Your abounding conceit, Major Mellen. Your pride
In subduing the feminine heart will abide
Any stabs you are likely to feel."

"Such sarcasm
Demands from somebody a fit cataplasm.
I go, Mrs. Lee, to receive it."

                          He bowed
Very humbly, and turned on his heel.
                                    "I've allowed
Major Mellen to say such unmerited things
Of my sex, that I really must silence his flings
In the future, I fancy," she laughing remarked.

They were silent a little; then all disembarked
For their dinner. A cool, grassy point that projected
From one of the islands was wisely selected,
In sight of the Lake of the Isles. There the trees
Made a murmurous music as stirred by the breeze;
The half-silence was sweet with the odor of flowers;
And pretty green islets, like shyly hid bowers,
Slept there in the sun, with their green garments
         trailing
The water that kissed them, and seemed as if sailing
Adown a green river to seas undiscovered
By mortal. Some saint of the beautiful hovered
About the rare spot, and enchanted it.
                                      Verily
Dinner out-doors should be eaten quite merrily
Ever; for half of the pleasure you take in it
Lies in the jovial mirth that you make in it.
Always some flies will get into the cream of it;
Fish that are frying will burn e'er you dream of it;
Milk that at morning was sweet has been learning
The secret of Nature that hints of a churning;

The butter that's "come" may have hastened by run-
    ning;
Mosquitos, persistent with bills, keep a-dunning;
The table is always a doubtful thing under
Its showy pretences, and causes a wonder
If crockery rests in a state of security;
Coffee goes down with a fear for its purity;
Seats are uncertain, and spiders abundant,
The ladies complain: there is nothing redundant —
That's quite beyond question — except it be fun;
But you almost regret when the dinner is done;
For the atmosphere tones up your nerves like a tonic;
The winds and the waves make a murmur harmonic;
You sit in the shadows, and see the wide world,
All its streamers of sunlight in splendor unfurled,
Roll along in glad glory to-morrow to meet,
And there's more in your dinner than merely to eat.

When this dinner was ended, they idled a while
On the banks of the beautiful evergreen isle.
Mr. Percival Trent, idling dreamily, laid
Himself down, like the dreamer he was, in the shade
Of a tree but a step from the others. To him
Was the cup of delight even full to its brim.
He had laughed and made merry this hour with the rest;
He would taste now the apples of gold that were pressed
To his hungering lips, — the sweet fancies that flitted
So bright through his brain.

"He has saddled and bitted
His Pegasus, certain," the major declared,
"And is off on a gallop. If any here dared
Overhaul him at present, I fear they would find
It a hard road to travel that's always inclined
To the Pisgah of dreams."
"I must say it were fitter
To speak of yourself, seems to me, as the bitter—
The bitter reviler of genius at times.
Did you try to reach heaven by a ladder of rhymes
Years ago, Major Mellen, and fail?"
"Mrs. Lee,
You are always a mild inquisition to me.
A few people were born with an interrogation
Curled up on the end of their tongue. Moderation
In questioning might be a virtue with these.
They are slow with their statements, but busy as bees
With conundrums."
"Some men never make a reply
To the plainest of questions," she said, "but decry
Every question that misses their lips. I was seeking
A reason why you should forever be speaking
So lightly of rhyme and its spirit. Success
In pursuit of a thing seldom gives to one less
Of respect for it."
"Well, you are free to impute
To me failure in wooing the Muse. To refute
Any false implication were idle indeed.

If my Pegasus proved but a slow-going steed,
And I early dismounted in common disgust,
I've a host of good company plodding the dust
Of our highway afoot. And I fancy the way
Of the rhymer, wherever his fancy may stray,
Is like that of the wicked : I think, my dear madam,
The path of the poet has known its McAdam."

"McAdam made hard what each Eve has made easy
Then, truly," she answered, with laugh that was
    breezy
And light. "I incline to the common belief
That the mother of poets is love, and the chief
Inspiration of rhyme is the sensitive heart. —
Is it so, Mr. Trent?"

                "You have guessed it, in part,
Mrs. Lee. If the rhyme be inspired in the least,
Then the heart or the fancy, by aid of a priest
Of the pen, must have wedded itself to the thought.
And some glow of true feeling is certainly caught
In the verse of the rhymer, when once it be found
With the laurel of true immortality crowned.
I believe there are volumes of rhyme written out,
As to which we may harbor a lenient doubt
If they ever were born of a true inspiration.
The art of mechanics has blind consecration
In person of some who would wear the green bays
Of the world's generosity."

GERALDINE.

"One of these days,"
Said the major with pride, "you may look for a poet
In *me*. When my heart is full swept, you will know it
By melody rare from its quivering strings.
As the swan must be dying when sweetest he sings,
You may know I have come to my absolute fate
When I utter the notes that are sweetest."
"The mate
Of the swan is the goose, Major Mellen, that misses
The music of better bred birds in its hisses
So sibilant. He that irreverent mocks
The rich note of a swan may produce a few squawks,
And betray his true species."
She took a delight,
As it seemed, in sarcastic allusion.
"I might
Pick a quarrel with you, my good cousin, for words
So sarcastic and cruel. Our mention of birds
Has evoked a whole flock of the turbulent daws
Over yonder, that utter their parrot-like ' caws '
Like a woman hard pressed for a sensible reason.
To give you back torment in kind would be treason
To gallantry, sore as I'm tempted. Alas
That a man is compelled to let ridicule pass
From a woman unanswered! To wish I were one
Of the privileged sex I could often have done,
Had I never remembered what one of them said,—
That, because as a woman she never must wed

Any woman, she even could feel reconciled
To her lot."
       " The good Montague painted it mild,
My dear major, for her. She was talking for men
To be pleased, and to quote her thereafter. And then
Lady Mary was vexed that the men should fare better
In marriage than women could fare."
          " I'm your debtor
Again, Mrs. Lee. Don't increase the large debt
By some stroke of your tongue more sarcastical yet.
Let us take to the water, like ducks, with a quack;"
And he nudged a good doctor near by. " To be back
At a sensible hour, we must speedily start."

All at once went aboard, and prepared to depart.
The main channel is narrow, that leads from the lake;
But a dozen make off from it soon, and partake
Of the tint of the little green islets. So deep
Is the hue of the streams, that the islands, asleep
On their bosom with verdure luxuriant, seem
To be part of them ever. You sail in a dream,
Winding in, winding out, in a labyrinth sweet
With the wood-blossoms thick in their silent retreat;
And you fancy that here, in its beauty supernal,
This calm afternoon is unending, eternal.

At length, when emerged from the river's glad maze,
They were on a broad channel, lit up by the rays

Of the down-going sun. Across yonder, Canadian
Hills sloped away in a beauty Arcadian;
Down the wide stream unobstructed, the view
Reached afar to the low-bending canopy blue;
On the right, close at hand, were the Paradise Isles,
With their loveliness spanning the magical miles;
Over all, the soft glamour of sunset, as calm
And serene as the peace of a hallowing psalm.

"The St. Lawrence is waiting its laureate yet,
Mr. Trent. With your words to its melody set,
It might come to its own by and by."
        There was ever
In Mrs. Lee's tone a mild flattery.
        "Never
Can measure and melody happier wed,
I'm afraid, Mrs. Lee," hesitating, he said,
"Than in Moore's little lyric of days long ago,
When he echoed the musical ' Row, brothers, row,'
Of Canadian boatmen. Its mellowing flow
I recall very often at twilight. He penned it
Not far down the river, whose placid waves lend it
A charm I shall never forget."
        "How could Moore,
Having seen the St. Lawrence, return to the poor,
Meagre life he had known? If you happen to learn
Why those poets who visit here ever return

To the feverish towns, will you tell me? It seems
To me certain that this is the river of dreams."

"Do men die in their dreams, Mrs. Lee? If they did,
Then the ruin and wreck of some lives would be hid
In a merciful way from their heeding. We live
As we must. 'Tis not all a receiving. We give
Of ourselves to the world, in return for its gifts.
Every hindrance or help that in some manner lifts
Us up nearer the ideal life should be held
For the good of our fellows. The hermit, impelled
To a lonely and selfish career, only cheats
His own being. His life is a canker, that eats
Out his soul. We may dream now and then by the way,
But to take on the armor, and fight as we may
When our respite is over."

"All poets, I thought
Till I knew you, were dreamers forever, and fought
But in fancy. You seem to be double: you carry
An active and passive that will not quite marry
In one; for you work and you dream, and do each
To the uttermost. What a magnificent reach
There must be and there is to your life! Do you feel
How much broader it is than the most?"

"Don't reveal
My conceit, Mrs. Lee, with your questions," he parried.
"I think that myself is quite happily married
To all that is in me. My labor and rest

Never trouble each other. My vigor and zest
With my indolence ever are fully agreed :
I'm as willing to stop as I am to proceed,
When a good time for stopping has come. And the
    scope
Of all life is the same, — from the fear to the hope,
From the doubt of the mortal, far on, till it holds
By the Infinite, where the immortal unfolds
Into trust. There is never a being more broad
Than to reach from itself to the merciful God."

After that, they were thoughtful and silent a while.
A rare flush on the sky held the grace of a smile,
As if heaven, bending over the earth in its sleep,
Saw a beauty to win it, ere pausing to weep
In the dews of the night, over sadness and sorrow
That darkened to-day, and must sadden to-morrow.
The evening wore on with much laughter and jest
From the others. The glow faded out of the west;
And the stars, in their marvellous shimmer and sheen,
Like a glimmer of glory, fell softly between
The old day and the new. 'Twas a time to be glad
In some quiet of soul such as he must have had,
Who, asleep on the plain, saw a ladder of light,
And the angels of God bringing peace through the night.

By and by they swung round, and across the broad
    sweep

Of the river below, as along the soft steep
Of the sky the late moon slowly climbed.
                    "It has been
A rare day, Mrs. Lee. If one never could win
His lost paradise back, had he known days like this
He could make for himself a few ages of bliss
Out of memory."
            "Woman lost Eden to man;
But he finds it again in her love."
                    "If he can,"
Said the major, near by, who had half overheard.

"If he *will*, I suggest as the much truer word,"
Mrs. Lee quick retorted.
            "Oh, well, he is willing
Forever, good cousin," he answered, "and thrilling
Quite often with sense of a paradise new,
But as often thrust out of it. Eves have been true
To their early example always."
                    "Mr. Trent,
Is there nothing can make Major Mellen repent
Such heretical speeches?"
            But Trent only smiled.
"He has nothing, in fact, to repent of. Such wild
And erratic assertions serve nought from his lips,
But to put for a moment his thought in eclipse,
As we all are aware. He's a genius for saying
What nobody doubts more than he does."

"But praying
The pardon of poets for trespassing thus
As a poacher upon their dominion, and plus
The humility even *I* feel to be found
By a poet himself on the privileged ground
Without proper consent, I would emphasize keenly
The right of all men to what poets serenely
Accept for themselves, — to exaggerate feeling,
Dissemble the thought they profess to revealing,
Make statements as fact that are half absurd fancies,
And build upon fiction their idle romances."

The major talked smoothly at times, with that flavor
Satirical still in his words.
     "There are graver
And guiltier crimes, Major Mellen, than one
You accuse yourself of, and then hasten to run
To excuses for ever committing it. Stay
In the poets' preserves quite as long as you may,
I can promise that they will forgive the affront,
If you bring us some game at the end of your hunt,"
Mrs. Lee made him answer.
     "Don't make game of me
In such cold-blooded fashion, I beg, Mrs. Lee.
We are near to the landing, let all disembark
Before you shall cruelly fire the whole park
Of artillery light which is hid in your speech:
There are others, you know, who might be within reach."

So with laughter and jest the day came to its close
For them all far along in the evening. Repose
Was as sweet as the day had been rare, and the vision
Of dreams that it brought had a beauty Elysian.

X.

AFTER this, there were days upon days of delight
Unalloyed. Percy Trent wrote to Geraldine quite
An unselfish account of his generous pleasure.
"I find in mere being," he said, "such a measure
Of happy content as I never have dreamed
When away from your side. Never gladness so gleamed
In the sunlight, as simply perennial seems
To one lingering here on the River of Dreams,
As the bright Mrs. Lee christens it. It is queer
That herself and the major should chance to be here
The same season with me. I am glad that they came,
Though their purpose and mine are not nearly the same.
They are here just to lose a few weeks out of life:
I am dreaming, the better to bear in the strife
A man's part by and by. It is well to recruit
For the battle to be. It is well that the lute
Should hang silent a while, that to-morrow its song
May be clearer and truer, more certain and strong.
Major Mellen is much as he was long ago,
Only bitterer grown in his speech; but we know,
Who have known him the longest, how much that he
    feigns

To be earnest is said for effect. That he pains
Me at times with his cynical sneers, I admit,
Notwithstanding; and often I laugh at his wit,
When I grieve with a hurt that is sudden and keen,
For he spares not the holiest things. He has seen
Some experience sad, I'm persuaded, — more sad
That its influence seems to be lastingly bad.
He was always a doubter of every thing true,
As a fact, or in word. 'Give the devil his due,'
After all; and the major has many good traits.
He is capital company often, and hates
Every sham with a hatred that urges assault
Of the fiercest. I fancy, at times, that his fault
Of condemning the right has grown out of long seeing
So much of the wrong and the false, and of being
So keenly alive to pretence.

                      "Mrs. Lee
And myself are the best of good friends, if to be
Always frank and outspoken together, to find
Satisfaction in similar moods of the mind,
To have sympathies somewhat in common, may make
Us all that. She has known, I am certain, the ache
Of a heart that is strong in its passion, unfolding
Its riches with never a thought of withholding, —
The pain that I fancy some women must keep
Throughout life, in a poverty wretched and deep
That was born of their prodigal love. Is there balm
For such aching of soul? In the liberal palm

Of the white hand of Peace, is there quiet and rest
For such throbbings of pain in so troubled a breast?
I am syllabling questions I only have thought
Hitherto. Though quite often with her, I have sought
In no manner to learn what her sorrow has been —
What it has been, perchance what it is. I begin
To be reverent even in presence of souls
That have hidden away in their silence the scrolls
Of their own revelation. No idle perusal
May learn of the secrets they hold in refusal
From men.

    "I suspect Mrs. Lee knew the arts
Of a finished coquette, and made playthings of hearts,
In some earlier time : there's no hinting, however,
Of conquest to-day in her social endeavor.
She treats all her friends in a courteous way
That is pleasant to see ; but I think she could play
A sad havoc with feelings the tenderest still,
If to times opportune she but added the will.
Do I hold her the less in respect for believing
She may have been guilty of ruthless receiving,
Aware that she could not give back in return?
It is true that I might, if I yet had to learn
That a woman wrongs man just to gratify her
Present mood, not to scarify him. I demur
But the least to her pleasing herself, if the hurt
She inflict be not truly malicious. A flirt
Who should send a man off into grimmest despair,

Just to see him writhe on in his agony there,
I would simply despise; but a woman delighting
Herself with the winning of love, and inviting
Its largess for pleasure it gives her alone —
Why, her motive might partly, in my view, atone
For the harm growing out of her deed. For of right
A man owes to your sex all the wealth of delight
He is able to pay.
     "Do you smile at my reasoning?
Well, you will pardon a moderate seasoning
Of the absurd in my argument. Those
Who are victims of feminine art, I suppose,
Judge more harshly than I do concerning it. You,
Who so easily might have made many to rue
Your attractiveness, ought with compassion to look
On another who possibly some time forsook
The true heights of her womanhood, found the low plane
Of coquetry, and made of her beauty a vain
Ignis fatuus, leading some men to their grief.
I have half been inclined to the foolish belief
That the major has suffered from Mrs. Lee's lack
Of requital in fullest degree; that far back
In his younger young manhood he loved her, as men
Like himself are not apt to love ever again.
And why not? They were friends long ago, it appears,
In a friendship that not very seldom endears
To the uttermost one or the other who feels it.
If sensitive yet from the hurt, he conceals it

Remarkably well, it is true ; yet a stoical
Nature like his may be truly heroical,
Smiling despite of its pain.
      " But you care
Very little for him or his past, I'm aware :
I'll not speak of them further. And as to my present,
I own that I find it so wondrously pleasant,
I would not consign it to yesterday soon.
The fair land of the Future may yield as its boon
Such another rare season of beauty and bliss ;
But I doubt if I find it hereafter in this."

So he gave himself up to his rhapsodies mild
When he wrote of the river. Its beauties beguiled
Him to frequent extravagant speech. That his eyes
Saw no every-day beauty with aught of surprise
She knew well. Was there loveliness for him so rare
As alone to enchant him thus utterly? Fair
As the River of Dreams might appear in his sight,
Could it thrill him to keenest ecstatic delight
With its beauty alone? Did no presence apart
From inanimate things take a hold on his heart
As with masterful sweetness?
      If questions like these
Were in Geraldine's thought, by the slowest degrees
Did they syllables take, and then ask to be heard
Of her love. And no query of wonder, no word
Of inquiry, escaped her to him. It was well

That he linger thus long at the Islands to tell
Her of beauty and blessing they yielded him.   So
She made answer in brief, and was glad in the glow
Of his gladness, without a foreboding or dread.
She could trust, and would trust to the end, she had said;
And the end must be well, let it bring what it would,
Since a Father so loving and tender and good
Had its shaping and care.
      There are natures that keep
Such a faith in such wise; but, if moved to the deep
Of their possible doubting, the tempest that rages
Within them so wild there is nothing assuages
But words of the Master, with tenderest thrill
Speaking out through the darkness their "Peace!"
   and "Be still!"

XI.

They had dined at Deer Island, a dozen or more
Of the seekers for pleasure. A half-shaded shore
Gave them welcome; its turf, that was mossy and sweet,
Running down to the water to welcome their feet;
And its trees, that were sentinels faithful and strong
Of the years, breathing out a monotonous song
Of old summers departed, half song and half sigh,
And inviting them listless and dreamy to lie
In the quivering shadows when dinner was done:
So they lingered in happy abandon. The sun,
When they took to their boats, had sunk low in the west,
And the night would be moonless; the river's fair breast
Was resplendent with ripples of silver and gold
As the breezes sprang up, and, with dalliance bold
And with passionate kisses, beguiled its repose
Into sighing unrest. They were near to the close
Of a glad day together, — these two we have traced
In their talk and their feeling a while.

"It's a waste
Of fine weather to think of returning so soon,"
Mrs. Lee made remark. "And this whole afternoon
Has gone by like a dream. *Do* I live, Mr. Trent?

Do I verily sip the sweet cup of content
As it seems that I do? Is regret but a thing
Of the past?"

"Into seasons like this not a sting
Of old memories ever should enter," he said.
" Let the dead of your yesterdays bury its dead ;
Drink the cup of content with no lingering glances
Behind. There is joy in the present. Romances
Forever abide in the future. Look out
On the shall-be as I do, with never a doubt
Of its bringing the best of your being."

He lifted
The oars as he spoke, and they silently drifted
Adown the still stream.

" Do you never feel fear
Of the future?" she asked. " Do you never seem near
To some terrible tragedy? Are you so certain
Of good you could lift the invisible curtain
Of years with no tremor of heart?"

With surprise
He looked deep in the depths of her beautiful eyes
Ere he answered, —

" My friend, you are keen at divining
Some thoughts unexpressed ; for I have been inclining
To fear of my morrows of late. And I stand,
As I fancy at times, on debatable land,
Between gladness and grief. In these days of delight
I am far up the mountains of being, in sight

Of that Beulah where grief is unknown; but I know
There are valleys of Baca through which men must
    go
Ere they climb to the summits of blessing. I wait
With a painful expectancy, early or late,
The upwellings of fountains of bitterness. When
They appear, I must drink, as do all other men."

"And some women," she added: "indeed, you might
    say
And all women. The waters that flow by the way
Are as Marah sometimes."
                    "There are few, I believe,
Who drink only the sweetness of life. But to grieve
Over sorrow gone by is not worse than to shrink
From some possible sorrow before. We must drink
The full cup of to-morrow, whatever the draught;
But, or bitter or sweet, it is not to be quaffed
Till to-morrow presents it. Sufficient indeed
To the day is the evil thereof; and the need
Of us all is a present of glad satisfaction,
Where nought of the past makes unhappy exaction,
And nought of the future repels or dismays."

"And you live in the present?" returning his gaze,
"Altogether, I mean, with no pain of the past
Throbbing up, and no glamour of happiness cast
On the days that are coming?"

                                        He smiled a reply
Before speaking.
                    "My patient confessor, if I
Should admit that I look for some gladness supreme
In the future, that, doing to-day, I but dream
Of endeavor the proudest to-morrow, 'twould seem
Contradictory.   I have admitted the truth,
That I fear in the future some possible ruth
Full of peril to peace; that I shrink from my morrows
In doubt.   But the future is broad; and it borrows
A radiance often from glories that crown
Us with gladness to-day.   And I never look down
The long vista of years, without seeing beyond
All their possible gloom an illuming as fond
As the kisses of dawn on the world.   I am glad
Of some day that's to be.   If one morrow prove sad,
I shall come to another, please God!"
                                        "A glad faith,"
She responded.   "But what of the past?   Does no
        wraith
Of some buried desire ever enter your room,
As you sit in the silence of solitude's gloom,
And torment you with words of regret?   You have said,
'Let the dead of your yesterdays bury its dead.'
Do your dead never walk?   Is there never a ghost
Of dead love or dead hope to intrude when you most
Would forget that you ever had hollowed a grave?
Does your past sink away, as this shell in the wave,

Out of sight, out of mind?" and she tossed a bright shell
She had held, in the water.
                        " No funeral knell
Has been rung in my past," he responded with feeling,
His sympathy touched by her sudden revealing
Of hidden emotion. "I've stood by no bier
Of my love or my hope. I can sit with you here,
And can say that my past has been pleasant and good;
That my present you make, as but one other could,
Satisfying, complete." And he noted the glow
Of a tenderer light in her eyes, and the flow
Of a deeper tint into her face. "I regret
Only duty ill done. I can never forget
What is gone, let it be whatsoever it may;
Not the less would I live as I should in to-day,
But remembering yesterday only for smiles
That it gave" —
            "Seeing somewhere the paradise isles
Of your dream by the sea?" interrupting him.
                                    "Yes,
Looking out on the billows before, I confess
In the faith that beyond their unrest there is calm
For us all in the infinite islands of balm."

"Will you teach me your faith? I am hungry for hope
In the years. With the greatest of griefs I could cope,
Could I only believe that beyond it is bliss.
You have much to make glad: there is much that I miss,

And but little I hold, and of this you have given
The most. On the wings of your friendship I've striven
To mount where the lark of your happiness sings:
I am weighted too heavy, I fear, for the wings,
Since I cannot fly far, and each flight only brings
Its discouragement."

      " Would I could lift you with me
To the heights of a happy content, Mrs. Lee!
To do this, my dear friend, I would cheerfully give
Half a year of the life that is left me to live."

She but smiled at his words.
      " I doubt not, my dear friend,
You would give, quite as freely as others would lend,
All you have — but the one thing you cannot."

         " And that?"

She was silent a little, and motionless sat,
Looking into the depths of the shimmering deep.

" Is a love that is tender and strong, that can sweep
Me up out of the gloom with its passionate grasp,
And then hold me content in the quickening clasp
Of its sunlight, — the love of a masterful heart
Full of power, most learned in the delicate art
Of its loving, most tender and loving indeed
When its pity could see there was bitterest need —
Such a love as a man gives one woman in life."

"And God pity him, then if she be not his wife,
Or may not be!" he said with quick fervor.
         "And she
Who so needs such a love, in whose heart there can be
Such a hunger without it?"
        "God pity her too,
In his infinite love, as all loving souls do!"

There were tears in her eyes as she questioned: each word
Had a thrill that was strange as he answered. She heard,
And was silent again for a moment, averting
Her face from his gaze. Sudden passion asserting
Itself in his breast, like a prisoner beating
Against the hard bars of his prison, entreating
For liberty, moved him beyond his control.
He was swayed by a tempest undreamed of. His soul,
Looking out of its windows of feeling, saw only
Another soul, helpless and hopeless and lonely,
And groping so after some path to the light
And the cheer he could give as he must. In his sight
She was near to the heights he had named. He could
  lift
Her to peace and content by the plenteous gift
Of his love, that was giving itself as if now
It had first love's sweet charity learned, — to endow
Needy being with riches untold.
        Ere he broke
Into utterance wild and vehement, she spoke.

"I'm but one of a thousand who hunger and thirst
For their manna in Egypt; who wander accursed
In a wilderness dreary, forever unblest
By the gift of that land which they should have possessed
But for doubting and fears. I shall die in my Edom,
And know not the gladness of faith that is freedom,
And service of heart that is scripture the sweetest.
My lot with the heathen Egyptian were meetest,
Unled by the Moses of love toward a land
I may never behold."

"When I gave you my hand
As your friend, Mrs. Lee, I had little to offer
Of worth, as I said; and, if now I should proffer
Such love as you speak of, it might seem as meagre
To you." He spoke low, with an emphasis eager
And quick. "*Could* I lead to the plenty that lies
Beyond Edom? My soul in its solitude cries
For companionship such as it never has missed
Till this hour. In the silence I tremble and list
For your answer."

She looked in his eloquent face
With a hungering look that will ever have place
In his memory, tears overflowing her cheeks.

"You must hear how my heart in its gratitude speaks
A reply that my lips cannot utter. Its throbs
Are so strong, they would shape all my words into sobs,
Did I try. As the call of a bird to its mate

That has lingered too long, and is home-flying late,
Even winning and tender as this is the cry
Of your soul unto mine ; and as glad would it fly, —
This poor shivering soul that is silent so long, —
Full as glad would it mount to the summits of song
With your own by its side, as when, night-shadows gone,
The glad warblers will wing themselves up to the dawn
In a sunburst of music. My comrade and friend,
Could you walk with me now, from this day to the end,
You could be — ah, how keenly I feel it and know it! —
Both heaven and the way. But you cannot. The poet
Within you may pity my need ; and the man,
In his passion of feeling that generous ran
To my help, may give all that he hath, even this
That is treasure the greatest of all : but the bliss
Of possession can never be mine. Do not ask
Any reason. For you I have lifted the mask
Of my heart, and you see it all quivering here,
As none other has seen or will see it."

                                    " So near
Have I come, as you say, my dear friend, to your side,
To be put thus away? Let whatever betide,
You must linger a while in my love. You have waited
Too lonely and long for the comrade belated
By fate, to repel him, or bid him farewell
With a half-recognition. My passion must tell
Its sweet story yet over and over again
In your ears. I must give you with lips and with pen,

As a prodigal gives, of the wealth of my heart,
Till you go from your poverty gladly apart,
And I wander a pauper forever, unless
You are prodigal too in return. I would bless
And be blest. May I not?"

       So he pleaded, the strength
Of his passion possessing him quite, till at length
It had mastered him utterly. Could she withstand
Such entreaty?

   "My friend, when you gave me your hand
As my friend, you gave much to a beggar for much,
And your friendship had in it a hallowing touch
That uplifted. My life had been swept passion-clean,
As I thought. In my desert no budding of green
Could give beauty again, I believed. You have shown
My mistake; but not less must I wander alone
Through the wilderness ever. Some manna is mine
By the way; and this day's is the nearest divine,
And the sweetest, that ever my hungering soul
Has made feast of. If only such generous dole
Could be mine through the years!" with a passionate
  thrill
Overflowing her speech.

      "As it can, if you will,"
He persisted.

    She shook her head sadly.

        "No more,
If you love me. But see! we are far from the shore,

GERALDINE.   103

And a storm is approaching." And as she thus spoke,
On the twilight's dim silence a thunder-peal broke,
And aroused him.
   Quick over the north there had spread
A black gathering mass, that grew dense overhead
While he looked. A dull moan was borne out on the air
From the pines in the distance. The day, that was fair
As a vision of peace, had departed in wrath
That would quickly envelop them. Straight in the path
Of the storm they were floating, as stoutly he bent
To his oars without answer, and rapidly sent
The light craft o'er the water.
    "Some shelter we'll find
Over yonder, I think, if we do not much mind
What it is," by and by he remarked. "It is plain
That the deluge will come very soon. We must gain
Any harbor that offers."
    He rowed with his might,
While the storm, sweeping on with the speed of the night
That it deepened too early, was nearing them fast,
And they heard the wild shriek of its trumpeting blast.

XII.

A MAGNIFICENT picture he saw as he rowed:
On his left, in the west, there yet lingered and glowed
The last rays of the sun, in a light that was yellow
As gold, and suffusing the sky with their mellow
Effulgence; the clouds coming nearest were red
As the crimson that flows from the battle-field's dead,
And above them were opal and purple and gray;
To the north, moving forward in martial array,
Were dense masses of darkness, and through them the
    flame
Of the lightning burned swift ere the thunder-peals came
With their torrent of sound. Far away, where the
    sky
In the lap of the hills appeared closest to lie,
The black mass became silvern; for rain had begun
In the valley beyond, where the lingering sun
Threw its light on a lower horizon.
                              On swept
The dark masses above, while the silvern sheet kept
Its way slower and gentler below, like a veil
Slipping down o'er the world in compassion. The gale
Would be on them before they could land, so it seemed.

More intense grew the darkness o'erhead; brighter
    gleamed
The mad lightning, more frequent its flame; all the west
In a moment was shrouded in shadow. The crest
Of each wave, as the water grew wilder apace,
Led the swift-flying boat on a wearying race
For the shore. Yet the strokes of the rower were strong,
Though he wearied. The storm was at hand; but the
    long
Way was over at last, as he lifted the skiff
Half its length on the sand, at the base of a cliff
Not too steep for their climbing.
                        "I'll draw up the boat,
So the waves cannot easily wash it afloat,"
Nearly breathless he said, as he helped her alight.
"There's a cottage here somewhere, I'm certain, which
    might
Give us shelter the best, could we find it. The island
Is small, I imagine. We'll climb to the highland
And see."
        So they bent their steps upward, her hand
In his own. On the highest uplift of the land,
In the midst of a grove rather scanty, appeared
A low cabin untenanted. Even this cheered
Their endeavor, and led them a welcome to seek
From its shelter uncertain. The door offered weak
And quick-conquered resistance. They entered as down
Fell the rain in a flood.

"We're not likely to drown,
Anyhow, Mrs. Lee, though the prospect is dark
As when old Father Noah set sail in his ark.
How the floods of our deluge unsparingly pour!
Hear the winds and the rain as they bellow and roar
Through the trees! See the lightning that blazes
    above us,
As if the dear Lord had forgotten to love us,
And came to us now in his wrath! It is worth
A day's wetting to witness him visit the earth
In the might of his power."
                        She shuddered, and drew
Herself nearer in dread. A fierce thunderbolt flew
Past their sight, and a crash, as if worlds in collision
Had met, fairly stunned them. An instant their
    vision
Saw nothing; their senses had gone with the glare
Of the lightning that vanished in gloom.
                        "Let me care
For you tenderly once, as I can," he appealed,
As he felt her form tremble. "There must be concealed
In the cabin some helps to your comfort."
                                He made
His way round in the darkness, now deep, till he laid
Eager hold on a rickety chair, which he brought
For her use; and, on searching still further, he caught
By the gleam of the lightning a glimpse of a cot
And a campstool.

"I own that these quarters are not
What they might be for cheerfulness," gayly he said;
"But there could be worse fortune than this that has led
Us to shelter so dismal. Imagine us yet
In the tempest out yonder! We never should get
To the land with our lives."

"'Twould have seemed little matter
To me only yesterday. Life did not flatter
Me much with its promise, although I confessed
To a horror of death. There was nought I possessed
Of a value worth counting. God's beggars have riches
Far greater than mine. I had torn from their niches
My idols of cost; and my heart's wide Valhalla
Was empty."

"And now?"

"You have seen the white calla
Unfold all its treasure of purity soon
As the morning blooms full in the sweetness of noon?
Even so has my love for you burst into bloom
From its bud in the dark. It would seem as if gloom
Must forever be brightened, indeed, with its light;
And to-day I have riches untold in the sight
Of this love that is mine."

She was speaking in low,
Suppressed accents, that took indescribable glow
From the feeling that moved her. He knelt by her side,
As a reed in the breath of her speech.

"You denied
Me the right any longer," he answered, " to plead
For the sweet privilege of supplying your need
To the uttermost. All that I am is your own
To do with as you may. Will you give me a stone
Of denial again, when I ask for the bread
Of possession complete?"

She but rested her head
On his shoulder in silence, her heart throbbing fast
As did his. In possession too perfect to last
He was hers, she was his, for the moment. He held
Her supremely his own; and his passion compelled
Her glad kisses in answer to his.

"But a taste
Of the honey of Canaan is mine in the waste
Of my wilderness barren," she whispered at length.
"It has marvellous sweetness."

"And marvellous strength
Has this love that I give you," he said in return.
"I believed I had nothing of passion to learn"—

"As did I; and the ratio of this that I feel
Fairly frightens me. Many a wife would conceal
Such a fervor of love from her husband; and I
Can be never your wife, Heaven pity me!"

"Why?
What shall keep us apart? You were made for my
  holding,"

He passionate said, almost fiercely infolding
Her close in his arms. "You are mine by the claim
Of my love, and your ample return. You became
Wholly mine when confession you made of that love;
And I hold you by right and by title above
All beside."

"It is madness to let you forget
Your own ties in this manner. Before we had met,
You no longer belonged to yourself. Could I keep
What another might prove to be hers, and so creep
By and by between me and my claim?"

Not a word
Of reply for a little escaped him. She heard
In the stillness between the loud thunder his heart
Beating heavy and quick, saw the color depart
From his face as the lightning shone on it, and felt
That he suffered. He rose to his feet where he knelt,
Put her tenderly from him, and strode to the door
As if panting for air. It was minutes before
He made answer in fact; then his voice sounded broken
And tremulous.

"Yes: I am glad you have spoken
Of what I should first have remembered. I thank
You for doing it, since I so wickedly drank
Of the cup of forgetfulness. Ever its flow
Must entice me, I fear.

"A few moments ago,"
Coming to her again, "my dear friend, I was mad

As the veriest lunatic. Passion has had
Its free run for a season. It may not outlive me:
It may, to my sorrow. No matter. Forgive me
For offering what was not mine to deliver.
Forget, if you can, what was said — on the river
And here. Let us be the same friends we have been
In these days of delight, if we can. Let me win
My good comrade once more."

      And she gave him her hand
With a clasp that was warm.

      "You are noble and grand
As no other man living could be," she declared.
"In your madness, if madness it were, I have shared:
Let me share in your penitence, too, Mr. Trent;
Though I doubt if indeed I do truly repent.
It was such a sweet madness! it thrilled heart and brain
With such gladness of being! it stilled all the vain
And unsatisfied longings that trouble my breast,
With such tremulant stilling to such a glad rest!
I shall love you — I must — though I never may tell you
Again of my love; and could loving compel you
To leave all the world, and to cleave unto me,
I should never indulge the compulsion, but flee
From your presence at once. For again let me say,
I must journey through Edom alone. If the way
Be so rough that I stumble and fall, you may pray
In the strength of your faith for my faltering feet,
That they carry me soon to some rest that is sweet;

And if prayer can avail one whose faith, in eclipse
By her doubt, is lost sight of, I'm certain your lips
Could efficiency lend it for me. But alas
For the wilderness lonesome through which I must pass
From this day to the end!"
        In the darkness he knew
There were tears on her face, and he tenderly drew
Her again to his arms.
      "I can be to you much,
Though I may not be all," he responded. "And such
As I freely can give you must freely accept.
Let what loving has sown, in the future be reaped
In our friendship. To walk by your side as your friend
Now and then, you must grant me from this till the
  end."

"Between you and my life," she made answer, "there
  lies
A great gulf that is deep as the ocean: our cries
For companionship cross it. You hold me, as here,
In the arms of your love, with your heart beating near;
But we stand far apart on the opposite steeps,
And between us there bide the impassable deeps.
Do not ask me my riddle to read. Let me hide
It away from you now and forever."
         She sighed,
And he answered her but with caresses, then rose,
And in silence peered out in the dark.

"I suppose
We must manage to stay here till morning. The rage
Of the storm is subsiding; but I can't engage
To return you in safety before. We are far
From the Bay, and there's not the first gleam of a
    star
Through the gloom. 'Twould be folly to think of my
    finding
Our way up these channels so many and winding
In darkness like this. I can make you a bed
On the cot yonder somehow, it may be," he said
By and by.
    Then he busied himself at his task,
With some show of success.
    " 'Tisn't all I could ask
For your comfort," he briefly explained, as he made
His way cautiously back to her side. " With the aid
Of a blanket or two, and a pillow, I think
You could rest very well. As it is, do not shrink
From accepting the best present poverty yields;
And be certain my tenderness watches, and shields
You from harm."
    " I *am* weary," she answered, " and glad
Of whatever you offer. No fair lady had
Truer knight for her service in chivalry's time
Than will guard me, I know. You should weave into
    rhyme
So romantic an episode truly as this is."

He pointed her words with some lingering kisses
By way of good-night, and then led her across
To the couch.
    "No: the world must submit to the loss
Of our living romance altogether. I hold
It a thing far too sacred for pen to unfold,
Even under the veiling of fiction. And then
You remember my thought, — that the poets don't pen
Their experience often."
     "Oh, yes! I remember.
You make of each poet a perfect dissembler,
Pretending to what is unfelt, and denying
The feeling he has any voice, only sighing
In secret perhaps. If I state it too strong,
Pray forgive me."
    He laughed.
      "But I own that the song
May be real to him while he sings, though in fact
It is fiction the veriest. Singers have lacked
Less in feeling, indeed, than in fancy. Poetical
Genius the finest, I fear, is heretical
Most with regard to the truth, rather shaping
What might be than telling what is; sooner draping
A dream in the garments of beauty, and making
Men think it of bone and of muscle, than taking
A skeleton out of the past, and with aching
Remembrance so robing it round as to show
What perfection of form fell to dust long ago."

" But I don't half believe in your theory, though
You do talk so convincingly sometimes about it.
One day, I am certain, you'll even half doubt it
Yourself. For you poets are men of rare feeling:
You *must* be, indeed ; and to think of concealing
It always is mockery. Even the claim
That your feeling flows out in some fiction the same
As in positive sorrow I cannot believe.
Men may weep at some fancy of grief ; but they grieve
To the uttermost only when sorrow cuts deep
To the quick of their souls. And we know, when we
   weep
At their words, what the hurt is. The mass of us feel
The same hurt, it may be, but can never reveal
Its keen torment because we are dumb. Why is speech
So denied to the many? Why is it that each
Of us has not the gift of expression? And why
Must some hearts go through life with a hungering cry
For the good that they miss, and unable to tell
What their need is, their hunger, their thirst? Is it well
For the world that so many are mutes?"
         " I'm unable
To answer, my friend," he replied. " What a Babel
Indeed it would be, though, if all were endowed
With a gift as of tongues, and at once the whole crowd
Should begin to communicate ! Angels defend us
From fate so disturbing ! May kind fortune send us
A quieter morrow to die in !

"Complaint, —
Speaking soberly now, as in fear of some saint
Of the silent departed, — complaint might be all
That from lips of the many incessant would fall,
Were they dowered with speech.   They might never
    give voice
To their hope or their faith; they might never rejoice
In some pæan of gladness to lift the heart up;
They might never in song press a cheer-giving cup
To the lips of those fainting and worn in the strife.
And the best of all song is the song that is life
To the dying, it may be, and strength to the weak,
And sure faith to the helpless, who only can seek
For some help far beyond them."
            "Yet song that is mellow
With tenderest feeling, that shows us a fellow-
Heart throbbing with ours in our need or our pain,
Has its mission, though born of complaint that was vain
And unworthy. Our sufferings syllables take
Of the words of the poets, and solace their ache
With a half-revelation in language our own
As we make it so only. No soul sings alone
In its loneliness truly; no other soul sighs
In its bitter regret, without hushing the cries
Of some near one unseen, but who pauses to hear,
And in silence is comforted."
            "Doubtful, my dear
Mrs. Lee. It's a pretty conceit; but I fear

It is rather too fanciful. Song may uplift;
But complaint is depressing. The true singing gift
Should be his who will sing in the world but to gladden it:
Dirges, indeed, may be sweet; but they sadden it.
All I could ask for my Muse would be this:
That it cheerily sing till some being shall miss,
When it ceases, a hope and a help, and shall long
For the singer's return, his renewal of song."

"But the sweetest of singing has ever a sigh in it;
Loving seems always to linger and die in it;
All that we catch in the syllables clearest
Is just a remembrance of what was the dearest
And nearest to some heart in days long departed."

"You've listened, no doubt, till the foolish tears started,
When he who so tenderly sang was but grieving
In fancy alone."
   "Is there, then, no believing
The word of a poet?"
   "Well, now, I suppose
If the word be spelled out in good truth-telling prose,
You may take it," he answered with laugh that was
  light.
"But I beg of you stop your conundrums. Good-night!
Get such rest as you can."
   "Will you give me a word
For my dreams that is sweetest the air ever stirred?

GERALDINE.

Say you love me, and say it in prose, that I never
May doubt it."
"I love you, shall love you forever,"
He said with low emphasis.
"Thanks! I could rest
Anywhere, anyhow, by such benison blest."

Then in silence he sat till the morning, his mind
All a tumult of troubled emotion. Be blind
To his wretched position no longer could he.
There was Geraldine Hope: here was Isabel Lee.
He was far from them both as the night from the day.
He was far from his faith as forever are they
Who forever are faithless. And so self-accusing,
Unspared of his conscience, and grimly refusing
To smother the stings that it gave, looking out
On his future with only a harrowing doubt
Of what might be in store, he awaited the breaking
Of day.
Mrs. Lee was asleep; and forsaking
The cabin when on the horizon a priest
Of the dawn began incense to burn in the east,
He walked down to the water his boat to prepare
For departure. No traces remained anywhere
Of their landing. Till sunrise had silvered the dawn
He made search without finding: the frail craft was
    gone.

XIII.

WHEN the rest of the party returned to the Bay,
Hurried on by the tempest that threatened them, they
Were surprised and alarmed to discover that two
Of their number were missing. But nought could they
    do
To determine what fate had befallen the twain.
To go out and make search in the storm would be vain
As unsafe.
        "They have landed, and there must remain
In such shelter as chances, wherever it be,
Until morning," the major remarked. "Mrs. Lee
Will regard it romantic. It may be that Trent
Will consider the storm as an episode sent
For his special advantage. He likes the dramatic
In life, and was always a trifle erratic
In love. He may die a true Romeo yet
In some desperate strait for the last Juliet
Of his fancy."
        And so Major Mellen, satirical,
Spoke of his friend.
        "If love shows us a miracle
Ever," he went on to say, "it is when

It renews itself over and over again
In the breast of a poet. So often it rises
Afresh from the dead, it no longer surprises
With new revelations of being. Besides,
It so largely increases itself, and divides
Of its multiplied measure so freely, it shows
Arithmetical qualities few would suppose
Could belong to a thing sentimental."
         The sneer
Of the cynic half hid, half revealed itself here
In his words.
    "Percy Trent is in love with my cousin
As madly as ever he's been with a dozen
Before; but he hasn't discovered the fact
Altogether, I think. When he does, he will act
Very much as if he had committed the sin
That has never forgiveness. He never would win
For the sake of the winning: he never would share
Of his love where he ought not, if caution or care
Could prevent it. His creed is the best; but the fact is,
His principle doesn't quite wed with his practice.
Don't blame him! I can't. Every man for his creed
Is responsible. Let that be right, let it read
Parallel with the preaching that seems to be best;
And society answers for him for the rest.
What he is, what he does, is small matter, so long
As the thing he believes is not glaringly wrong.
Then the heart is indeed a free agent: the head

Cannot hold it in humble subjection. If led
Into ways that are wicked, no part of the blame
Should be thrust upon him who gives only his name
To the agent, and does not control it. Whose love
Is within his discretion? Whose will is above
His affection, directing and guiding it? Better
That hearts should love often than always be debtor
To prudence for perfect restraint."

        So he ran
To his flippant, irreverent speech, that began
To be reckless at times.

        The next morning shone clear
As the mornings that dawn in the blush of the year.
Major Mellen, denying his habit, forsook
The seduction of sleep. Rising early, he took
His way down to the wharf, thinking haply to meet
The belated pair on their return, and to greet
Them with playful reproach. But his keen vision scanned
All the channels in vain, to the dim-lying land
On the Canada side, far away down the stream.
The wide waters were tinted with morn's rosy gleam,
And unflecked by a sail. The white flash of an oar
In the sun was nowhere to be seen.

        Long before
His late breakfast, the major was anxious, but laughed
At the fears of the rest.

     "He can manage his craft
Like a riverman born," so the major contended.

"If out in it when the quick tempest descended,
He'd safely enough make the shore. He's expert
With the rod and the line. They have come to no hurt,
But are breaking their fast in poetical leisure,
Perfecting a bass in a broil. There's a pleasure
For poets in cooking the fruit of their lines,
As in eating it, under the odorous pines
Of a solitude wild. Trent would hardly desire
To be known as a monk; but a very good frier
He is, I am certain — of fish. They will fare
Well enough till we see them again as a pair
Of meek truants returning to school."

                                      Yet he made
Sudden haste to secure the small yacht, nor delayed
To set out on a mission of quest, when at noon
The twain missing were still unreported. As soon
As the search had been fairly begun, he confessed
To himself an untimely delay, and, impressed
With a fear undefined, he kept watch as they sailed,
Half in hope, when they came near the shore, to be
    hailed
By the ones whom they sought. Every island they
    rounded,
Each headland they scanned, until hope was confounded
With keen apprehension in all. Not a trace
Of the boat or its burden appeared. The broad space
Of the river below the last islands was crossed
And recrossed yet again, to make sure that the lost

Were not hinted of there in some manner; and then
They went farther above. As they rounded again
A small island that could not a shelter have given,
The major caught sight of a skiff that had driven
Itself on the rocks.
                "It is Trent's!" he declared,
With excitement that each of the company shared
As they neared it. "And stove to a wreck! We have
    found
All we shall for the present. They must have been
    drowned
By upsetting last night in the storm."
                                    And he grew
Quickly pale as he spoke. When they landed, he flew
In hot haste to the boat; but it offered no clew
To their seeking, beyond its bare presence. It lay
Without oars, bottom up, badly broken.
                                        The day
Was far spent when they gave up the search, and re-
    turned,
Bearing with them the cast-away skiff, having learned
Nothing more. No one doubted the common conclusion
Expressed. They had perished. To hope was delusion.
Their bodies, if found in a day or a week,
The sad truth could not even more certainly speak.

The gay world at the Islands made proper lament
For the hour; and a thrill of true sorrow was sent

Through some hearts when the story was told. Before
    night
The quick lightning had spread it abroad ; and its flight
Was a message of sadness to many.
                               One read
In the papers next day, with a black-letter head,
Just a brief paragraph ; and it soberly said,
" Mr. Percival Trent, as a speaker well known,
And his friend Mrs. Isabel Lee, out alone
On the River St. Lawrence last night in a squall,
Were capsized, and were both of them drowned."
                                    That was all.

XIV.

The one reader knelt down in the pitiless gloom
That came over her soul, as if sudden a tomb
Had enveloped her there, and in syllables broken
Besought the All-Father to send her some token
Of love and compassion to show her that still
She could bow to his power, and suffer his will,
Though it crush her, because for the best.
         It was long
In the dark of her doubt, ere she caught the faint song
Of her faith once again, like a bird that sings low
In the shadows, before all the world is aglow
With another glad morning. At first she gave up
To her grief unrestrained. Of the tear-tasting cup
She drank deep, till its bitterness flooded her hope,
Overwhelming it. Long as a life did she grope,
So it seemed, like a person struck blind in the sun,
Seeing nothing.
     "O Lord! if thy will must be done,"
She could only beseech, "in this terrible way,
Take me also to thee in thy mercy, I pray.
I am wicked and weak and unworthy, but hear
To my pleading, O Lord, I implore!"

If the ear
Of the Infinite ever were open to all
Who in sorrow's unreason thus bitterly call
For the end, or if, hearing, he answered the cry
Because merciful only, full many would die
With their life in the bloom of its purpose. But God
Is as wise as paternal. He spares not the rod
Of affliction, however he loves us. Denying
The answer we seek, he is touched by our crying,
And gives, in the time of his wiser replying,
The answer to profit us most.
     Yet we plead
In the midst of our want for some possible need
We believe to be ours; and we hold empty palms
Up to God, while we cry for particular alms
At his hand; and the boon that we seek might be
 worse
For us ever than poverty's bitterest curse.
Very blessed indeed are the poor, when they crave
What would hinder and hurt, if the All-Father gave
Without stint to their asking. More blessed are those
Who in praying remember the All-Father knows
Of their need even better than they, and bestows
With a wisdom divine.
     It was pitiful, first,
To see Geraldine clinging to all that was worst
In her grief. He was dead, her one lover, — as true
As the heart that so bitterly mourned him, she knew.

He was dead, and thus ended her dream.　She could
　　never
Again feel his tender caresses.　Forever,
Till death gave him back, so her sorrowing said,
She must hunger for love, and be ever unfed.

By and by — she could hardly have told if a week
Or a day had been passed in the gloom — she could seek
For disguising of comfort.　　　　Death gives us some things
For our absolute holding, that might have found wings,
And been wafted beyond us ; and so Death is kind.
What he gives us, we keep ; and if tears make us blind
To the gift, and we see but a grave or a bier
For a little, we come to a vision more clear
Later on.　Then we know that this token of Death
Is immortal ; that never of this can the breath
Of regret say with sighing, "O change of the years!"
That we never shall go with lamentings and tears
On a wearisome search for the lost.　What we hide
In the peace of the grave will forever abide
In its promise and grace, in its beauty and truth
For the mortal is age.　Immortality's youth
Can know nothing of age, or of change, or decay.
It has never a morrow of fear.　Its to-day
Of content is eternal.　　　　A glimmer of light
Came to Geraldine out of the dark of her night.

He was dead, her one lover; but thus he was hers
Beyond shadow of doubting. No dimness that blurs
Any distance could come between her and her own.
They should never be separate. Weary and lone
As her future might seem, he could never be far
From her life and her love. No distrusting could mar
Their companionship now evermore. Not a hint
Of unfaith could be heard through the years. Without
  stint
She might give of her heart to his memory fond,
And forever be glad in the giving beyond
Any possible shade of regret. Death had set
The great seal of its silence on lips that were yet
Full of utterance tender and true, and had stilled
With its marvellous hush the heart-throbbings that
  thrilled,
And must thrill to the end, for herself.
        Could it be
That this woman of women, this Isabel Lee,
With her heart in her face, and her love in her hand,
Might have won him away with her witchery bland?
Could it be that some passion to flame might have fanned,
That he never had dreamed of, asleep in his breast?
Could it be that his love for herself, in the test
Of some crucible heat in his life, might have burned
Into nothingness? Might he some lesson have learned,
With the wisdom of love making wiser his heart,
In which previous knowledge had never a part?

If a question like these sought reply in her grief,
In its possible doubt was a certain relief.
If the sorrow so keen had been sent but to save
From a sorrow far keener, the hurt that it gave
Was the touch of a hand hurting only to shield:
In the pain of its purpose there lingered concealed
A sweet comfort to gladden and bless.

           The allies
Of our happiness come to us oft in disguise,
And we think they are foes. They are not as they seem,
And we welcome them not to their mission supreme;
But we turn in despair from besetting so sore,
And would flee, if the way were but open before.
Then we wait, as we must, in the struggles that keep
All our being in terror, and out of the deep
Of our peril we call for the succor delayed.
In some day of clear vision we see there was aid
Where we knew but assailing; and then, in surprise,
With our gaze lifted up to the peaceable skies,
We behold from our peril and pain a release,
And are glad and content in the triumph of peace.

XV.

AFTER searching in vain the small island around,
Where no hint of the object he sought could be found,
Mr. Trent to the cabin returned. Mrs. Lee
Was awaiting him.
  "Breakfast for you and for me
Must be late," he remarked but half anxiously. "We
Are two castaways now, without means of support.
For a little we promise to be but the sport
Of such fortune as comes to us."
  Then he explained
How their boat had been drifted away. It remained
For them only to wait for some vessel in sight
Or in hail, to be signalled, or told of their plight,
When deliverance quickly would come ; and meanwhile
They must comfort themselves in the comforting smile
Of the day, that gave sunlight to follow the rain,
As the morrow will always.
  He smothered the pain
At his heart, and made merry with laugh and with jest
As if never a dread of the future oppressed
Or appalled him. His passion he met with resistance
Begotten of struggle with self ; and a distance

Indefinite, infinite, widened and grew
Like a desert between them.   Instinctive she knew
He had conquered himself for the time.   No regret
For the past or the present his scrutiny met
As he gazed in her beautiful face ; but serene
She looked out on the blue of the sky, and the green
Of the islands, and moulded her mood to his own.

So they waited and watched till the morning had grown
Into mid-day, and patience with waiting had flown.
They were out of the track of the steamers that plied
The American channel : it happened, beside,
That no boat from the Canada ports came along
Until noon. When it came, on its decks were a throng
Full of riotous mirth, on a pleasure-trip bent
To the village some miles from the Bay ; but they lent
Ready ears to the call for assistance, and sent
Speedy means of relief.
      "I can land you at Berne,"
Said the captain, who hastened their story to learn,
When they stood by his side.   "You can dine there,
  and go
To the Bay when you please.   It's a moderate row
Of three hours, and the boatmen are plenty."
        And faint
With their fasting, no longer inclined to complain,
They but languidly noted the beauties abounding,
The merriment over the still water sounding,

And heeded but little the comment they caused.
When at length the slow steamer reluctantly paused
At a rickety wharf, they went gladly ashore,
While the vessel backed off, and its proper course bore
Farther on.
   Man is mortal. There's nothing so tells
Of mortality, nothing so certain repels
The romance of our being, the essence and spirit
Of life, as the hunger that feeds it. Men fear it,
And flee it; and yet in their folly they nurse it
With spices and tonics, till wretched they curse it,
And die of dyspepsia and doctors. The greed
Of the animal dominates over the need
Of the heart and the brain. And all sentiment waits
Upon hunger; is happy or hurt as the fates
Of the stomach decree. The day's measure is dinner.
Man loves like a saint; but he eats like a sinner,
Forgetting his love till his appetite flies,
But remembering well when capacity cries
To be spared.
   At a quaint little inn they were greeted
By fare not too fine, when at last they were seated
Before it. But hunger for diet the meanest
Gives sauce that is lively, and relish the keenest.
They ate as if love were a manna untasted
In wilderness ways; as if hearts had but hasted
Their good to forget, or the lingering pain
Of their sorrowful hurt in a marvellous gain.

By and by they were ready to leave. Sweetly slept
The wide reaches of water, unstirred, as they stepped
In the skiff Mr. Trent had obtained. Like a mirror,
The river reflected the sky, that seemed nearer
Than ever to brood o'er the world. As serene
As a picture of peace was the beautiful scene.
The mid-afternoon sun, swinging low in its place,
With an autumn-like glory suffused all the space
Round about them. The far-away hill-tops were crowned
As with silver. " Be still ! " said the silence profound
In suggestiveness sweet to the ear of the soul:
"For the troubled in heart there is always a goal
Of content. Mother Nature, with tenderness blind
To the faults of her children, and ever inclined
To give gladness for sorrow, invites them to lie
In her arms while the tumults of being surge by.
She invites them in quiet and comfort to rest,
From all weariness free, on her pitying breast;
And Jehovah, in loving and tender accord,
Says, 'Be still! and discover that I am the Lord.'"

There are times to be silent, — sweet seasons of calm,
When the soul seems to catch the soft breath of a psalm;
When the Infinite lifts up the finite, and bears
It away from the lowland of troubles and cares;
When we rise to a holier being, supernal
In good and in blessing, with fields ever vernal,
Where bloom the dear blossoms of beauty that hide

From our happiness lower, where vistas are wide
As a world for enchanting our rapturous gaze,
And we look from our height with delight and amaze.

It was little they said as they floated away
Through the silence serene on their course to the Bay.
If the mood of the scene had not swayed them, the feeling
Of each must have counselled to partial concealing;
But above their own moods was the mood of the hour,
And it silenced their speech with a mystical power
That they could not divine. Yet for Percival Trent,
Though the time was so full of supernal content,
There was under it all, half unheeded, the ache
Of a heart that has made the one bitter mistake
That must ruin its peace evermore. When he rested
His eyes on her face, he would gladly have breasted
The billows of fate but to win it and hold it
His own, to look into it ever, to fold it
Henceforth in his loving embrace. But a boat's
Length between them, the limitless ocean that floats
The great treasure of continents, sundered them far
By its pitiless waves; and Hope flung not a spar
For his seizing, on which he might drift till he held
Her to him, unresisting, forever. Impelled
By the currents swift rushing around him, he knew
He must call to her through the wide reach his " adieu."

He must float wheresoever the wild waters bore,
Though no haven he find on a rock-bordered shore.

The short, slow, lazy strokes of their boatman were swift
To their longing desire. 'Twould have pleased them to drift
In this quiet so tranquil forever. No haste
Of the world was upon them. To linger, and taste
Of the lotos-blooms thus, till forgetfulness came
With its blessing of peace, who could chide them, or blame?
The long day was approaching its close when they neared
The hotel. To a few who there sat, they appeared
As if raised from the deep; but before the news spread
To the many, that these were alive whom as dead
They were mourning, they both slipped away out of sight.

From a sleep that was restful and soothing that night
Into which he had sunk upon reaching his room,
Percy Trent awoke late, and arose in the gloom
To look out on the river's broad bosom. The glimmer
Of moonlight, just gilding the trees with its shimmer
And sheen, gave a color and glow to the dark;
And when, later, the moon had ascended the arc
Till her beams fell in fulness, as soothing and tender

As sleep was the glow of her affluent splendor.
Yet restless and troubled did Trent linger there
By the casement to gaze on a picture more fair
Than the day, to be bathed in a glory more rare
Than the noon's, but with bitterness thrilling his heart.
Then he sat himself down, and besought the shy art
Of the poet to soothe.   Thus he pencilled

APART.

Beyond the sea, beyond the sea,
In some fair land to dream of thee
To-night, my darling, would I be!

No softer breezes there might blow;
No sweeter music there might flow;
No moonlight there more tender glow.

My dreams might find no rarer bliss
Than here they yield on nights like this,
Wherein no richness do they miss.

Throughout the glory and the sheen,
The sunset and the dawn between,
No fairer picture might be seen.

On all the evening's quiet rare
No benediction, as of prayer,
More sweet and calm might linger there.

But waking, when the night was done,
To dawn of day and rise of sun,
To life and thought again begun,

Methinks 'twould comfort bring to me
To know between my love and thee
Were reaching leagues and leagues of sea;

To feel that distance real and wide
Were keeping me from thy dear side,
The sunlight of thy smiles to hide;

To know that days must come and go,
And moons must wax in cycles slow,
Before thy presence I could know.

But here to-night the moonlight glows,
And while the breeze so balmy blows,
I seek in dreams a sweet repose.

It comes with restfulness and peace;
It brings my soul a glad release,
While all my doubt and tumult cease.

Yet waking, with the dawn of day,
My heart will see thee near, and say
"Good-morning, love!" and bid thee stay.

Then, as through distance, thy reply
Will come, like breathings of a sigh,
Or accents of a sad good-by.

"Good-morning, love!" thou'lt answer me;
But more than leagues and leagues of sea
Will separate my life and thee.

XVI.

The next morning he copied his verses, and sent
Them to Isabel Lee with this message: —
                              "I meant
To take leave of the Islands to-day — and of you:
To depart from your presence without an adieu
Or a word of farewell was my purpose. I've staid
Far too long as it is. But some talk will be made
On account of our recent survival: I'll tarry
A day or two longer, and help you to parry
The gossiping comment I helped to create.
Thus I give my excuse for delay to the fate
That would force me away from your side.
                              "When I go,
It will be to a future of struggles. I know
What is duty. I know I should say my farewell
To this month of delight with no feeling to tell
Of my treason to love so long plighted. Distrust
Of my manhood may come when I see, as I must,
To what pitiful weakness I early am brought.
I may wonder, perhaps, if when I shall have fought
The hard battle, and won, this poor sham of a life
Will be worth all the effort, the struggle, and strife.

Yet I know what is duty, and, knowing, shall walk
In the line of it steady and brave, though it mock
Me with bitter denial of strength. For we grope
To the altitudes highest when being and hope
Are in deepest eclipse by some fate unforeseen :
So I comfort myself with the shadows between
My blind path and the sunlight shut out.

                                                " A defender
Of right should not wave the white flag of surrender
When wrong his position assails, though the wrong
Come beguiling to peace with some snatch of a song
That is pleasant to hear. And the wrong of this passion
Of mine, that has come in such innocent fashion
To capture and hold me a captive, must feel
The quick arming of conscience within me, the leal
And unyielding resistance of manhood, to meet
And make combat against it. I know, I repeat,
What is duty, — my duty, — and, knowing, abide
By the knowledge. Henceforth in the past I will hide
What is past ; and my present shall be — what it can.
For the future — well, being is brief ; and the man
Who gets through it the soonest in manliest way
Has the happiest ending.

                                          " The major might say
Something very like that, to be sure ; but his quarrel
With life than my own is more ancient : the moral
Of which rather pertinent fact is, that he
Should be reconciled rather, and leave now to me

The most bitter complaints about being. If I
Am inclined to turn cynic, and utterance try
That is doubtful and reckless, remember the stroke
That is stabbing my soul to its quick. If I spoke
As I feel, I should shock you with bitterest speech
That a sane man could utter. But lips that can preach
Wise philosophy e'er must be careful, and frame
Only language discreet, though the heart be aflame
Just below."
    To which message she speedily gave
A complaining, pathetic response: —
        "You would save
Me the pain of farewell. Let it be so; and when
You depart on the morrow, as commoner men
Hold my hand for a moment in theirs while they speak
Their adieux, you shall clasp it as if in a week
You might take it again in your own. And return
When you will, soon or late, — be it soon! — you shall
  learn
How my heart has been keeping its tenderest things
For your welcome; shall find with what gladness it
  brings
The poor offering up to your altar, and waits
For some look warm with loving to cheer the hard fates,
And to kindle the ashes to flame. With your pledge
To remain as my friend, I can stand on the edge
Of this wilderness where I am walking, and seem
To catch glimpses across to the land of my dream;

Can forget for a time with what bitterness all
Who are shut out of Canaan must hunger and call,
Mid the flesh-pots of Egypt, for good that they miss.
You are not to deny me your friendship; and this,
If it tenderer be than the many could give,
If it nurture itself at love's fountain, and live
Thus a life that is warmer than others may see,
Shall be beauty and brightness and blessing to me.

"Duty takes you away for a while, so we'll phrase it.
And duty — we're given to foster and praise it;
But ugly enough it can be, and as hateful
As sin. There is nothing in life quite as fateful,
Or so I believe. I am sick in my soul
Of its bitter exactions. The costliest toll
That we yield on the highway of being is paid
To these, whether we will it or no. We are laid
Under tribute, indeed, to a Cæsar who claims
All we have, all the best of our longing and aims;
And we give without hope of appeal. Do not wonder
I put the case plain and with feeling; for under
This cruel oppression of duty I cry
In a poverty wretched for riches gone by,
And no answer.
                "To-day we shall meet as do those
In whose soberer veins never surges and glows
The warm current of passion; shall trifle with speech
As if never the heart underneath could beseech

For a clear revelation in word, as if lips
Were commissioned, indeed, to put thought in eclipse;
Shall be careless, untroubled, and gay with the rest,
Though a riotous tumult may stir either breast
To pathetic, unspoken appeal. So we play
At the mirth that is mockery mad, and obey
The mad will of the world, that would bid us conceal
What the will of our hearts would so gladly reveal.
We shall meet as they meet who have little to gain
In the meeting, no deep-stirring pleasure the pain
Of their yesterday's parting to stifle; no burning
Unrest through the brief separation; no yearning
For glance of an eye, or for touch of a hand,
Speaking language that love may not misunderstand.
Let it be so. I'm used to all bitter restraint
Upon gladness and warmth that can make the heart faint
With repression and hunger. No bitterest trial
Henceforth can be harder than this of denial
That through the long years I have helplessly known.
I should say that my heart must be hardened to stone,
If it were not that now, as I think of you here,
I can feel its quick throbbings.
      "You may not be near
In the flesh: in the spirit you cannot go far
From my side, though you go the world over. We are
As apart as are darkness and day, though we walk
Arm in arm a day's journey. So distances mock
At conditions, and laugh at desire. So the flesh is

Divorced from the spirit it feebly enmeshes,
And twain they must be evermore."
           As he read
Her response, to his feverish longing it said
More than syllables strongest could utter. It throbbed
With the pain and the passion behind it that robbed
Her who wrote of her peace. In its silence it spake,
Even more than its speech, of the wearying ache
Of her soul. It aroused all his sympathies, strong
And intense as his love, to the uttermost. Wrong
As it might be to stay, he was tempted to bide
The results of a wrong very sweet by her side,
And remain; for she needed him. Hunger like hers
Can be fed by one bounty alone. It occurs
To those wealth-giving hearts only, born to make gift
Of their riches unchecked, to go out from their thrift
Into want such as this. So he reasoned. He knew
That his need of her, born but with yesterday, grew
Every hour. Could he smother it, crush it, and kill it?
Is hunger a thing to forget, if you will it?
Will want, lean and wolfish, grow comelier there
If you sit in its presence and fancy it fair?

When they met, half a hundred were hearing her tell
How the storm came upon them. She pictured it well,
And in spirit dramatic. How many could guess
That her language, so fitting, and free to express

The alarm of the moment, the peril and stress
Of the time, was a mantle to cover the feeling
Far deeper? that words so intense were concealing
The incident's actual color and glow?
That the mood of that night never mortal might know
Save herself and the man whom she greeted as one
Of her commonest friends when he joined them?

"Well done,
Good and faithful," the major declared in his light,
Flippant way. "Though you gave us a horrible fright,
We forgive you. But don't undertake the heroic
Again with this cousin of mine. She's a stoic,
I grant, and would make not a word of complaint
To be cast away often, if only some saint
Of romance would invoke with his kind benediction
Such company pleasant; but harrowing fiction
So very romantic too pungently savors
Of fact."

"We will spare you such odious flavors,
I think, in the future," said Trent. "Mrs. Lee
Is as patient as any lost Crusoe would see
His companion in trouble; and none could desire
Better company, should he unwisely aspire
To the life of a castaway. One such experiment
Answers, however. There's not enough merriment
In it to make us demand an *encore*.
We are satisfied quite, without crying for more."

"I supposed you were fond of positions dramatic,
And might not object to one slightly aquatic,"
Said Mellen, satirical. "Poets are pardoned
For tastes rather perilous. Fancies have hardened
Their sensitive shrinking from facts. The romantic
In dreams should not render them foolishly frantic
If coming to active reality. Most
Of the guild, I suspect, would incline to make boast,
Soon or late, of a thrilling and strange episode
So uncommon as yours, in an epic or ode."

"Now I warn you to spare us your comments derisive,
For once," Mrs. Lee with a manner decisive
Declared. "You would make of an epic or ballad
One element only of bitter-sweet salad
For cynics to feed on, who'd say grace with sneers,
And would smile in derision at sentiment's tears.
You who laugh at poetical things of romance,
And so boldly charge at them a-tilt with your lance
Ever drawn, are so many unwise Sancho Panzas,
Because you could never pen passable stanzas
Yourselves, and so win the world's plaudit for wages.
The prose of our being has many dull pages:
The poetry of it is none too profuse,
And each incident striking, I think, has its use.
What this recent adventure of ours may have meant,
I am puzzled to tell; but perhaps Mr. Trent
Will some picture find in it to grace, by and by,

The one poem each poet ambitious should try
To embalm himself in." And she laughed.
                              "From such banter
A Pegasus modest would flee at a canter,"
He parried. "Mine dare not remain." And he bowed,
Self-possessed and amused, to the gathering crowd,
And betook his way down to the river, his heart
Strangely stirring within him. The marvellous art
Of the woman he loved, in so meeting with grace
Unconfused the demand of the time and the place,
Made him wonder. No woman beside, he believed,
Could have faced the surprise of the hour, and de-
    ceived
All who saw her and heard her so soon into thinking
The episode fruitless of love. Without shrinking,
She told all there was of that notable night
For the curious ear; and her silence was quite
Unsuspected concerning the holier things
He must set himself quick to forget; for the stings
Of his conscience were cutting and keen. The begin-
    ning
Of passion despotic was bitter as sinning
When sin has been drunk to the dregs. Now for him
There was only a fate full of wretchedness grim,
And to-morrow must usher it in. He would start
On the early boat, leaving at five, and depart
Without word of adieu. And this calm afternoon
He would seek for his spirit some balm-laden boon

In the quiet of channels none other might find,
Wherein beauty and redolent odor combined,
And where dreaming, aglow like the blush of a rose,
Should beguile the unrest of his soul to repose.

XVII.

The pale gold of the west into crimson had burned,
And then faded to purple, before he returned.
He had done more than dream in the hours intervening;
Had pondered half wisely and well on the meaning
Of passion so futile, so bitter, so rife
With the seeds of all bitterness, meeting his life
Where its path appeared gladdest; had wondered if so
Into every existence some mad currents flow,
Making turbulence where should be placidest peace;
Had questioned if ever this tumult would cease
That now troubled his soul; and had reasoned that being
Is only a cruel and blind unforeseeing
Of problems we never may find to be soluble.
Out with a friend, and inclined to be voluble,
Trent would have talked in the dubious tones
Of a man who has battled with fate, and who owns
To his utter defeat, who is idly indignant
With life and its lessons.   The beauties benignant
Amid which he rowed could not suddenly quiet
The feverish pulse that so boldly ran riot

Within him; no balmiest opiate breezes
Could bear him at once the glad blessing that eases
Tormenting thus born of some lingering bane.
Yet at evening he found himself back, with the pain
At his heart rather stupefied; found himself ready
To meet a gay welcome with nerves that were steady,
And voice that could syllable badinage gay
As the gayest, nor once by a tremor betray
Any deep hidden feeling.
     That night, as the few
Whom he daily had met, and thus pleasantly knew
In such casual way, were about to take leave
Of each other, he mentioned his going.
        "I grieve
To announce that good-night must be also good-by
In my own case," he said, "though I leave with a sigh
Of regret that the summer so nearly is spent."

"And you go in the morning? I think, Mr. Trent,
You should kindly have told us your purpose, that we
Might prepare for the parting," said Isabel Lee
With surprise well affected, her manner as free
From all touch of restraint, and as simply well bred,
As if never a tenderer word had been said
Between this man and her. "We shall see you again
Before winter?" she asked; and as commoner men
Took the hand she extended, politely he took it
In formal farewell, and as lightly forsook it,

Determined to show that he also could cover
All signs that might hint of his being a lover.

"Perhaps. I have promised a night in November
At L——, and may call at that time. I remember
My friends when I can," as if most to forget
Were his custom exacting.
      Some words of regret
From the others were spoken in courteous phrase.

"I may meet you in Rivermet one of these days,"
Said the major, with manner as easy and hearty
As if the brief sentence were not made a party
To eager suspicion, and wish to detect
Through the words, or their carefully noted effect,
Any reason for Trent's sudden going.
       Unshaken
And cool as the major himself, Trent had taken
His leave of them all in a moment, and stood
On the ample veranda alone.
      "Very good
As a piece of lay acting, that was, I admit;
But there's something not hinted, I'm sure, under it,"
Major Mellen remarked by and by to the major,
There being no other man near; "and I'll wager
A box of Havanas that Bell has been flirting
With Trent till he flees her with wound that is hurting
Him hard. She can stab with most delicate art.

Can it be that the girl ever had any heart?
What a marvellous actress she'd make! She had known
Of his plan for departure, of course, but has shown
An indifferent ignorance mighty well feigned;
And there's reason, I'm certain. The man had remained
Here a fortnight beyond his original date:
He'd have tarried a full fortnight longer, if fate
Had not shown him his danger. He'll shun Rivermet
And Miss Geraldine Hope till this fair Juliet
Be forgotten. And somehow you can't soon forget
Such a woman," he added, with grimace that spoke
Of unpleasant remembrance his language awoke.

" It is well that I quietly published my going,"
Thought Trent, as he looked on the river deep flowing
Before him, the night-breeze but tenderly kissing it.
" Were I without the least word to be missing, it
Might cause remark, and then gossip would say
There was reason peculiar for going away.
I suspect that the major, keen-scented, quick-eyed,
Some hint of the truth has already descried:
His allusion to Rivermet may have been wide
Of all purpose he had, except simply to see
If, in parting thus early from Isabel Lee,
I should hasten to Geraldine Hope. Having heard
Our reputed engagement discussed, it occurred
To him, doubtless, that I have been guilty of treason."
He felt his face flush in the dark, as if reason

Were ample for such an unpleasant impression.
"My self-respect once was my surest possession,
I fancied: I'm losing my grip on it fast.
Can a future of duty deep cover this past
So it cannot stare up at me pallid and white,
Like the face of a friend unforgiving, whom quite
I have killed with keen cruelty? Can I still live
My poor future so bravely, that self can forgive
The sad wrong I have done it, and lift up its head
As if shame were not living, and trust were not dead?
Yonder river runs tranquil and sweet as it glides
To the sea; but the ocean's unquenchable tides
Are but bitterness all. Do I stand on the brink
Of a sea as resistless and bitter, where sink
The sweet hopes of these earlier years? Must I sail
By the compass of duty, though borne by a gale
Of fierce passions to harbor unkind?"
        So he mused
And he questioned till midnight. His conscience refused
The short comfort of sleep until well toward the morn-
 ing.
He rose in good time for the steamer, and scorning
The pitiful weakness that so overpowered
His strength, and compelled him to fly like a coward,
He walked to the landing, and hastened aboard.

As he sat on the deck, the glad sunrise restored
Him in part to himself. He is wanton, in truth,

(Who is farther away from his age than his youth,)
Who can see the dawn flush, the horizon fast redden,
The color burn into the skies that were leaden,
The stars slip away into measureless spaces,
The mountains grow rosy and glad as their faces
Look sunward and catch the first smile of the day,
And not thrill with the glory revealed, and not say
In his heart a thanksgiving.
     The Islands quick faded
In mellowest distance. The sunlight, unshaded
By fleck of a cloud, or by film of a mist,
Lay across the broad river, and lovingly kissed
Every ripple to laughter and silence. A spell
Of enchanting content on the voyager fell:
From this land of the real all gladly he turned
To a country of dreams where they never have learned
To forget and be wise.
     And the day wore along.
When the quivering steamer dashed into the strong,
Angry sweep of the rapids, Trent roused to the scene,
And became, till it passed them, a spectator keen.
Did they typify being, *his* being? Must he
From the currents of peace irresistibly flee
To such wild buffetings? Was there nothing before
Like the beauty behind, where the rush and the roar
Of this channel tempestuous early should fade
Into murmurous music, Æolian made
By the harp of his memory?

Eager and swift
The boat flew to the beckoning billows that lift
Far above the sharp ledges at anchor beneath,
And that over a current so treacherous wreathe
Into sparkle and foam. In the swirl and the sweep
Of the waves, that so madly and merrily leap,
They went madly and merrily downward careering,
No anger of rock or of river once fearing, —
A spirited race as with water is run!

Where the silver St. Francis, asleep in the sun,
Smiled them welcome unworded, they drifted from sound
Into silence, — a silence as sweet and profound
As is midsummer calm, — and from struggle to rest.
So there come to our lives, when we stand the hard test
Of the billows that buffet us, reaches so still
That we drift in delight with the current's calm will,
And find peace. The broad lake of the river was smooth
As the sky overhead, and its beauty might soothe
Any trouble of soul. Far away on the left
The low spire of St. Regis in peacefulness cleft
The horizon of blue; far away to the right
The blue hills of the south faintly bounded the sight;
And before them the river's magnificence swept,
As the steamer straight onward her patient way kept,
To the narrower channels below. Here and there
A stray water-fowl, lazily beating the air,

Was the only suggestion of life beyond reach
Of the vessel itself: if the silence had speech,
It was only an echo of yesterday's life,
Or it hinted, mayhap, of some possible strife
Yet to be.
          As the sun was fast sinking, its flame
Of white heat into rosy red burning, they came
To the river's superlative charm, — the La Chine.
It is just a mad passion of waters between
Two long levels of tranquil repose.   The St. Lawrence
Here dashes the majesty grand of its torrents
Swift down the decline ; here it hurls them in wrath
High above the rough ledges that torture its path ;
Here it ripples and laughs, here it seethes and it surges,
As on to St. Peter's sweet quiet it urges
Its dangerous way ; here it dances and sings ;
Here it pours and it roars, and its wild current flings
Into spray ; here, with grandeur majestic, it sweeps
O'er its breakers, and smooth and unbroken it leaps
From the crest of the low cataract ; here it beats
Into fury along the sharp headlands, retreats
From its futile attack with the thunder of hate,
And renews it again ; here it flies to the fate
That awaits it, with passionate force ; here it lingers
As if it were clasping compassionate fingers
In loving farewell ; here it hurries and flashes,
And scurries and gleams, and in mad columns crashes
Against the high rocks that defy it insultingly ;

Here it springs over the ledges exultingly,
Breaks into foam, and goes merrily drifting
And lifting, and leaping and plunging, and shifting
From color to color, as if there were dyes
Of all marvellous tints where it flashes and flies ;
Here it lifts the stout prow that encounters it, sways it
With terribly masterful will that betrays it
Almost to disaster and death ; here you feel
A quick shiver of fear course along the boat's keel,
Till she struggles with pain like a person, and shudders
With live apprehension, and writhes in her rudder's
Strong hold, and leaps forward at length as if greeting
Her moment of mastery, heart and soul beating
With martyrlike purpose heroic : for here
She may sail with the sky bending over her clear
As a crystal, the winds in Euroclydon's caves
All asleep, and yet meet as wild tempest as raves
When the demon of storm his black anger has hurled
O'er the waters, and God has forgotten the world.

As he stood on the bow of the steamer, Trent saw
The smooth waters uplift, as if swept by a flaw
Of some wind that he felt not. A rift it appeared
At the first ; but as to it they steadily neared,
It grew angry and strong as the surf of the ocean :
He saw the wild channels in wilder commotion,
And heard their low thunder, more sullen and loud,
Like a warning to venture no farther. The crowd

Gathered round him, alert and intent. At the wheel,
The grim face of their pilot, with muscles of steel
Quick to answer command, was immovably set,
Looking into the torrent beyond. As they met
The first break of the water, a breathless suspense
Came upon them, a fear that no human defence
Could avail against madness like this.
                                    Through the leaping
And boiling and thundering waves they went sweeping
And surging, a sense as of rapidly sinking
Within them, a tardy and cowardly shrinking
From fury still madder to come. And yet faster
They swept through this turbulent hell of disaster,
Where ruin and wreck seem forever at home.
Through the billows of green and the breakers of foam,
Sinking down with a tremor and thrill o'er the ledges
Beneath, and careening far over the edges
Of cataracts highest, the stout vessel tossed
Like a shell in the surf, its swift course often crossed
By the outjutting rocks that so cruelly waited
To crush it, but always as happily fated
To shun its hard foes, and each moment confounded
By terrors yet greater.
                            The thunders resounded
In mightier music majestic; the leap
Of the waters was wilder and fiercer; the sweep
Of their desperate will conquered being and breath
As the gasp of the dying is conquered by death.

Still the pilot peered out on the tempest before,
Undismayed by its terrible tumult and roar,
And the captain stood silent and stern at his bells,
With a look as intense as if tolling farewells.
'Twas a mad, irresistible race with the devils
Of furious flood, where their turbulent revels
Are maddest, — a race to remember as glorious,
Once you have won it, and panting, victorious,
Through its wild pleasure and peril at last
To the tortuous channel below you have passed,
And you know by the quieter waters, serene
As the sunset, you safely have run the La Chine.

XVIII.

Trent remained for a day, but to pay the brief call
Of a tourist in passing, at gray Montreal;
Then uneasy, uncertain, he walked the boat's deck
That should land him next morning at quainter Quebec.
Until late in the evening he paced up and down,
Looking back on the walls of the vanishing town,
Looking out on the opposite islands low lying
In beauty of green, on the sky that was dyeing
Itself in the crimson and scarlet and gold
Of the sunset, with eyes half indifferent. Cold
To the color that warmed all about him, and glowed
The glad heart like a dream of the tropics, he rode
Through the lingering twilight, and into the dark.
The dim shores faded out. A late fisherman's bark
Came in call, and stole by like a ghost, with its sails
Wing-and-wing, as if wooing the slumbering gales.
Some hilarious raftsman, afar out of sight,
Let his lusty-lunged laughter float out on the night
Till it frightened the echoes. The passengers aft
Over gossip and story occasional laughed,
Till Trent listened in positive pain. He was lonely,
And longing, and heartsick, as they can be only

Who taste the one pleasure of life but to miss it,
Who pine for the face of a friend, when to kiss it
Would open the windows of heaven.
                                    He went in
The deserted saloon, compensation to win
For his loneliness there, if he could. Sitting down
To the open piano, he hastened to drown
His regrets and unrest in its magical flow.
To his delicate touch it responded in low,
Sympathetic sonatas, that lingered and thrilled
On the sensitive ear, or in melodies filled
With the wordless compassion of song. So he played
As the mood was upon him. Some quiet ones made
Their way in from the deck, and close up to his side;
But he heeded them not — or his manner belied
Any heeding. Enrapt in the harmonies rare,
He could easy forget every trouble and care,
All the common surroundings of time and of place.
Through the sweetness of song, some enrapturing grace
Breathed upon him its witchery soft, till he knew
Neither doubt, nor misgiving, nor dread. Thus he grew
To be soberly glad. Thus he sang, ere he ceased,
In a strain that the gladness of singing increased,
Of a lesson he learned from

THE LIGHT IN THE EAST.

I saw the day fade into darkness;
I saw the glow shade into gloom;

And I felt a great dread in my soul as I said,
  "Can the night bring a bud to its bloom?
Can there ever be born a bright morrow
  Of sorrowful dark such as this?
Will the sun ever shine with its glory divine,
  And the beauty and blessing I miss?"

I sat in my doubt half despairing;
  I knew not the way I should grope:
So I wondered and wept by my hope as it slept,
  And I feared it the death of my hope.
More deep was the darkness, and denser
  The gloom that enveloped me there;
And my faith grew so weak, it no longer could speak
  The sweet syllables shaping a prayer.

O Father, forbearing and tender,
  Have mercy on souls that are dumb!
To their silence reply through the dark, "It is I!"
  As in comforting love thou dost come.
The need may be deepest that cries not
  For lack of strong agony's word:
O Father, come near with thy comfort and cheer,
  And give answer as if thou hadst heard!

A bird singing low in the silence
  Brought healing for hurting to me:
For I saw, looking far by the horizon bar,
  What the sons of men ever may see, —
The gloom of the midnight departing;
  The day, from its bondage released,
Stealing up through the space, with a light on its face, —
  The glad, wonderful light in the east.

GERALDINE.

"The night of my vigil shall vanish,"
    I sang with the song of the bird;
"For the sun never set on a yesterday yet,
    To rise on a morrow deferred.
The dawn is as sure as the darkness,
    The pledge is as true as the boon;
For the light in the east never failed us, nor ceased
    To make certain the morning and noon."

As he sang in a baritone mellow and trained,
With a feeling and thrill that were deeper than feigned,
Many lingered and listened, and finally sighed,
That a song so beguiling and glad should have died
Into silence so soon.
                He arose and went out.
He had sung himself back into peace from the doubt
He had wrestled with so through the days. It might be
That the morrow would wound him afresh : he was free
From all weary besetments to-night. He could rest
In the darkness untroubled by dread, and possessed
By no fear for the end.
                The next morning the height
Of historic Cape Diamond first greeted his sight,
And above the gray walls of the citadel hung
The tricolor of Britain. A battle-ship swung
By its anchor, asleep in the harbor below.
The bright roofs of the city took dazzle and glow
From the sun but just risen. Without haze, or the fleck
Of a cloud, the sky shone upon silent Quebec.

When the steamer swung round in the channel, and swept
With some bustle and stir to her landing, he stepped
From the New to the Old ; for the centuries waited
Here once, and since then have been always belated.
As up to the gate from the river you climb,
You go back a long cycle or two into time ;
You see round you the life, and the works, and the
    ways
Of the world in its ruder and ruddier days,
When the color of being so readily run
To the surface, that battle and pillage were done
For the sake of the doing ; when war was a thing
To be studied and learned for the fame it should bring ;
When the shedding of blood was a part of Christianity,
Practised and preached for the good of humanity.

Please don't infer that they pillage and plunder
To-day in the sleepy old town ; do not wonder
If Trent beheld murder and rapine and lust
As in wars mediæval, where settles the dust
Of the past undisturbed on a present too quiet
To start a more valiant crusade than a riot.
I made, it may be, an unfortunate reference,
Too comprehensive and broad, out of deference
Only, in fact, to the city's antiquity.
History simply concedes the iniquity
To it, 'tis true, of repelling long sieges,
Defending the onset of loyalty's lieges,

Withstanding the shock of the enemy's hosts,
And compelled to see carnage unsought.
                                But the ghosts
Of dead heroes yet walk the high battlements round it;
Red fame has a place where men sought it and found it;
Still grim and defiant re-echo the guns
That in silence have slept through a century's suns;
In the cry of the sentry a dim challenge calls
Out of long-buried lips from the citadel walls;
The wild music of musketry breaks on the air,
Where the garner is death for the gallant who dare;
And above all the present's calm quietude reigns
The fierce tumult of strife upon Abraham's Plains.

Through the quaint, crooked city our friend made his
    way,
Searching out the things quaintest by night and by day;
Walking over the battle-field hard by the town;
From the parapets airy and bold, looking down;
Looking on at the garrison's showy parade;
Idly watching the pride and the fashion displayed
On the terrace; or bowling right merrily on,
Through the Gate of St. Charles or the Gate of St.
    John,
In a rocking *calèche*, to the country that sleeps
Beyond city and suburb at peace, or where leaps
Montmorenci in beautiful haste to be wed
With the wooing St. Lawrence. The life that he led

For a week was the life of a dreamer unstirred
By the impulse of action. He languidly heard
The faint callings of duty, and answered them not.
In the midst of such sleepy surroundings, forgot
Was the wide-awake being and doing so near
In his future. The lotos-blooms redolent here
He would press to his lips, and forget.
        But he failed
In forgetting. Regret his good purpose assailed,
And wherever he went he was haunted by thought
Of what had been and must be. His dreams ever caught
The sweet flavor of emerald islands, the sheen
Of the waves as they twain had long drifted between
In those days of delight, and his sweetest repose
Was a blessed remembrance.
        Most happy are those
Who have only remembrances blessed! who turn
From no memories bitter, with feelings that burn
Like a fire in the breast! They have come to the garden
Of paradise so without knowing it. Pardon
For sins of the past cannot blesseder be
Than, in granting forgetfulness certain and free
Of the sin put away, that henceforth it may never
Stand ghostly and grim by the present's endeavor,
And mock it, and make it afraid.
        Though the time
Was so full of a dreamy content, to the rhyme
Of each day a sad music was set, like a moan

Amid mellowest laughter, — a low undertone,
Never ceasing, half heeded, half heard, but existent,
And paining the ear of the soul with persistent
Continuance. Walk where he would, he could hear
The low pulsing of pain far away, and yet near
As the conscience within. He could never forget
To the full of forgetting, so long as Regret
Was his daily companion, rose with him at dawn,
And sat with him at eve when the twilight was gone
Till he bade her a weary good-night.
        At the end
Of a week he took up delayed duty, and penned
A long letter to Geraldine Hope. If it read
Like his former epistles, but little it said
Of the ardent affection of lovers, implying
What might have been written, in no wise denying
By evident lack what he often had told.
While he wrote it, in fact, if the love had grown cold
That he felt for her once, it was only, it seemed
To himself, by comparison. Passion undreamed
In its mastery, coming unheralded quite,
Had not hidden this older love out of his sight
As a thing very worthful and sweet.
        'Are degrees
With the heart so impossible ever? Are these
Who have burned the hot flame of fierce passion's desire
To its ashes, no more to be warmed by the fire
Of some calm-glowing feeling? Believe it who will:

You may sit by the blaze of your passion, and thrill
With quick grief as it flickers, and falters, and dies;
But some day from the embers new color may rise
Into glowing, and gladden you. Grieving is brief,
Or the sum of this being were simply a grief.

XIX.

"MY DEAR GERALDINE, —
              "Pardon unwonted delay,"
So his letter began, "in my writing. Don't play
At the brief indignation you never must feel
At my gravest shortcomings, nor try to conceal
The sweet fact that long silence has new revelation
Of need. I've been dreaming, and lacked animation
For more. That's the only excuse I can render.
There's something that lurks in the crystalline splendor
Of summer days here that I cannot explain;
It has proved, in my case, a most excellent bane
For the poison of purpose to do. I have drifted
From morning to night like the veriest gifted
Do-nothing of genius, — my only ambition
To see, and to feel, and be glad. If the mission
Of sunshine were ever performed as a healing
And free soporific, in balminess stealing
Through heart and through brain, and so lifting the weight
Of hard duty and care, it is here. How the late
Mellow twilights beguile to repose! How the calm
Of each morning seems pressing some opiate balm

On the eyelids! How earth in a beautiful swoon
Seems to lie through the glow of each brief afternoon!
How the far-away mountains are hallowed with rest,
As if truly the summits of God! How the west
Into marvellous color and majesty glows,
As the sun to his morrow magnificent goes
Through a gateway of gold!
      "You may say, if you choose,
I am florid in feeling. I never shall lose
Out of memory's life the week's rest I have known
Here in quiet Quebec. When I weary am grown
Amid duties to come, I shall dreamily drift
Out of bustle and crowd, to the holiday gift
A kind fortune has granted to have and to keep,
And be sweetly refreshed as if gladdened by sleep.

"Having been the whole round of the places historical
Here, I might now, in a style paregorical,
(Sleepy, you know, like the air of the town,)
And with guide-pages handy, proceed to put down
All the facts and the figures important. But no!
You shall wait yet a year, and come with me, and grow
Even wiser than I am concerning the place.
Do I see a glad flush stealing over your face
At the prospect so pleasant? I like the half-blush
That you wear at odd times, when you say I must
  hush
Some fond nonsense or other. You're prettiest then.

Do not show the same blush to less fortunate men,
Lest they envy me more!
　　　　　　　　"As for history here—
In the magical glow of to-day's atmosphere
There is little but being historic. And yet,
If I lounge on the Terrace when Fashion has set
Its gay current there soon, I shall see as much pride
As disports itself now on the popular side
Of Broadway, New York, in this day of our Lord
Eighteen hundred and blank. If I greatly abhorred
The Dame Fashion, I'd say with some bitterness mild,
She was wrinkled and gray, even history's child;
And I'd point you, in proof, to that notable twain
Who began their existence in clothes rather plain,
And became quite ashamed to be seen. But I'll grant
That the pride which so gayly would flutter and flaunt
The fine trappings of dress is a modernized thing,
And that over the picture the promenades fling
A bright hue of the present, to lessen and lighten
The half-sombre tint of the past, and to heighten
The picturesque whole.
　　　　　　　　"Yet you feel, when you stand
On the parapet yonder, as though in a land
Of dim yesterdays fled; and you walk the quaint street
As if certain some knight mediæval to meet;
And you listen to mass in the Jesuit piles
Of the priests, as if monks moved about in the aisles
From the far middle ages.

"Poor priest-ridden people!
If only there lifted some truth-telling steeple
To point the true way they must go! But the spire
Of the Jesuit never points heavenward much higher
Than head of the prelate or priest; and the soul
Of the dead or the dying must pay proper toll,
Or go seeking its paradise long. In this dreary
Sahara of doubt the one spot that is cheery
And vernal alone is the Virgin. Dear Mother
Of Christ! Because each, in believing, his brother
Becomes, we may hallow her thus with our love
As the mother of all; but before and above
The sweet mother Madonna forever is Christ;
And whoever from worshipping him is enticed
To a less adoration, while walking the way
Of a faith without fruitage, must penalty pay,
And not penance. Some paintings a worthy grace give
To the Virgin; but Christ as an infant must live
In the arms of the mother Madonna, or hang
From the cross where he died with the crucifix pang
On his face, as the Jesuits have it, instead
Of ascending on high, from his place with the dead,
And remaining a Saviour for all, with no need
Of a priest to stand up, and with him intercede
For the seeking and penitent.

"Battle-fields teach
Many lessons. The monuments on them may preach
A wise gospel that calls for no shedding of gore.

On the plains where the men of Montcalm fled before
The wild charge of their foes, is the legend, 'Here died
Wolfe victorious.' Life is a battle-field wide,
And we fight for the right or the wrong till the end.
I have wondered how many who fall, my dear friend,
Are the victors, how many go down to defeat,
Never gaining the victory certain and sweet,
But discouraged, disheartened, dismayed. Marble shaft
Never rises above them; no spring where they quaffed
The last cup of refreshing is pointed to those
Who still linger, and face the fierce onset of foes
That the world never sees; but they slumber unsung,
And are silent forever. God pity the tongue
That prays feebly for help from defeat at the last,
When it ought to be singing thanksgiving, as fast
It sinks down into silence! I think it were blest
Thus to die like this soldier of fortune, who pressed
To his lips a clear draught from the spring, and then went
Into rest, let us hope, with a warrior's content,
Having won. But he won as must all, having fought
Like a faithful and true knight of God. Had he sought
Cheaper victory, doubtless defeat would have robbed
Him of glory and fame. Never faithfulness throbbed
Out of life into death without recompense just,
Though it come when the heart is but ashes and dust.

"But I'll spare you philosophy further. Please credit
This much to the mood of my pen, that but led it
Astray.

"I have lingered here longer than most
Of the sight-seers do, who 'from pillar to post'
Hurry on as if fevered with haste. By and by,
In the sweetest of leisure indeed, you and I
Will thus tarry untroubled, unhurried, together,
And paradise find in this marvellous weather.
To-morrow I leave for the Saguenay, — far
Down the river, and up where the solitudes are.
I have made Montmorenci a visit to-day
For the last, and shall list to the exquisite play
Of its murmurous music no more, lest I listen
In dreams. Where its waters gleam ever and glisten,
Like showers of pearls in the sun, I have laid
Half the day full of dreamy delight. The cascade
Partly faces the town; but a leisure hour's ride
Down the river's left bank, yet unseen from the side,
You approach it. In front, between it and the stream
It is leaping to meet, is the vision supreme
Of its beauty. A green, grassy point there invites you
To linger and gaze, and with gazing delights you;
For yonder the play of the waters is sweet
As the sunlight that silvers the foam at your feet;
Their loud thunder has lost all its resonant ring,
And in murmurs Æolian softly they sing
Through the distance between; like white gossamer lace
They droop down the precipitous deep, with the grace
Of a bridal veil gleaming with gems. You could linger
In rapt fascination forever, the finger

Of silence laid soft on your lips, that you might
Ne'er attempt the expression in words of delight
Inexpressible.
    "Yonder, with beautiful smile,
The St. Lawrence sweeps onward, and kisses the Isle
Of Orleans like a lover, and fondly embraces it;
Turn half around from the falls, and one faces it, —
River of silver and island of green,
A pure emerald set in a circlet of sheen,
A fair picture of peace as man ever has seen.
On the opposite side are the cottages low
Of the poor *habitans*, an irregular row,
Running nigh to the dim water-line; far beyond,
In the yet dimmer distance, the sky bending fond
To caress them, the mountain-tops blend with the blue,
And your vision has bounded the reach of the view.
Turn again to the right and the west, and you gaze
On the slumbering city, its roofs all ablaze
In the sunshine, and flooding its soberer grays
With a tropical glory; its batteries, grim
And defiant as hate, become mellow and dim
In the distance; its rugged and angular steeps
Sloping gently and soft to the river that sleeps
At their base; and above, the red cross of St. George
From the citadel flung.
      "I have sat by the gorge
Which the point overlooks, so enraptured and charmed
By the scene, that my driver no doubt was alarmed

For his fare, apprehensive that I would attempt
To slip off as a suicide, going exempt
From the fees common visitors pay. As I staid
There to-day, and the fall sweeter melodies played
In farewell, I wrote thus of

THE SUNNY CASCADE.

Fair Montmorenci gleaming goes
 Adown its dim defiles:
In nooks no human vision knows,
Its tricksy current laughing flows,
 Flash out its silver smiles.

Far up amid dim mountain dells,
 It drinks from crystal springs:
Of cooling rills and mountain wells
It gayly sips, and gladly tells,
 As free it leaps and sings.

It lingers long in quiet grots
 Where bending birches weep:
Where bloom the blue forget-me-nots
Along the warm and sunny spots,
 It sings itself to sleep.

It wakes to laugh at foaming rift,
 And flies with merry glee
Adown the swirling rapid swift,
Where mossy walls in wonder lift
 Their whitening heads to see.

It sinks to rest by pleasant shades
  Where meadow-reaches run,
Or gleams coquettish through the glades
Where long it mirrored dusky maids
  Who dusky warriors won.

And rousing soon to rougher ways,
  It sports through rocky fen,
Where bright the sunlight streams and plays
Within the lonely woodland maze,
  And longs for haunts of men.

Then down the wider steep it flies
  With eager, hastening feet,
And sweet complaint for smiling skies,
To leap with laughter and surprise,
  And glad its wooer greet.

Serene the broad St. Lawrence flows,
  Yet winning with its smiles;
And Montmorenci gleaming goes
In joy to wed its sweet repose
  Where bliss alone beguiles.

Forever down its dizzy height
  The cascade sunny leaps,
Its waters robed in angel white,
Its song an anthem of delight
  From heaven's own azure deeps.

Its pearly spray, to diamonds kissed,
  Plays truant with the breeze;
And on it borne as lightest mist,
In flush of gold and amethyst,
  It seeks the sunset seas.

The fleecy foam in beauty falls
  To hide the bare abyss;
From out its dripping cavern-halls
A witching Undine laughing calls
  To win her lover's kiss.

And ever on in sportive race
  Fair Montmorenci runs;
Forever changing all the grace
That wimples on its smiling face,
  Yet changeless as the sun's.

"I must bid you adieu till each other we see,
When my roving vacation has gone, *vis-à-vis*."
And he signed himself brief, in a style that was meant
To seem loving as ever,
     "Your
        "Percival Trent."

XX.

MAJOR MELLEN had business or pleasure again,
Or it may have been both, down at Rivermet, when
He returned from his summer's diversion. He made
A long call upon Geraldine Hope, and he played
In the cruelest way with her peace. She acquitted
Him, true, of deliberate wish that admitted
Such torture to her: she could scarce have believed
That with purpose prepense he would idly have grieved
Her as now. She accepted the pain that he gave
With a patient acceptance, submissive, and brave.
And withal she was glad that he came; for he brought
A great blessing of comfort at first; and it caught
Her up, willing and weak, in the shock of its flow,
Overcoming her quite.
                    " I can never forego
Paying tribute to friendship as pleasant as yours,"
He remarked, " and the business is kind that insures
Opportunity easy. I'm barely returned
From the River St. Lawrence, all blistered and burned
By the sun, as you see. We have had a month's leisuring,
Filled running over with vagabond pleasuring,
Sandwiched with some of gay fashion's formalities,

Spiced with a few of flirtation's dualities.
Jolliest company, too, that I ever
Was out with, and rather uncommonly clever."

" You must have been fortunate, major," she said
As he paused, though she felt that the color had fled
From her face.
     " Well, I was: it's my normal condition,
You know," and he laughed, as if every ambition
He knew had been gratified. "When a man chooses
To waste a few weeks doing nothing, he loses
His temper as well as his time, if the rest
Who should aid him in laudable ways are possessed
Of the devils of social discomfort. They tear
Very many, Miss Hope, I am willing to swear
On the word of a man who has studied them well:
They are devils of which there's no record to tell
Out of whom or of what they were cast. It may be
They went down with the swine to their bath in the sea,
And escaped — with their piggish propensities, grunting
At every experience, always affronting
Your pleasure and patience. There can't be a place
That is better for lifting the mask from the face
Of a character rude than half-roughing it where
The good-humor and fun are a part of the fare.
There were none in our set with whom grumbling was
   chronic;
No one of us bored all the rest with Byronic

Quotations and sentiments; nobody flung
A wet blanket of sneers from the loom of his tongue
Till he chilled the whole company; all were discreet
And good-natured, forbearing and wise, as is meet
For a party of idlers like ours. Even I
In deportment, I fancy, was rated as high
As the others — unless it was Trent."
         As he named
Her belovèd, it seemed he had purposely aimed
A keen arrow to enter her bosom. She gasped
As if panting for air, and convulsively clasped
Her hands close in unheeded beseeching.
         "He carried
The honors off easy — or would if he'd tarried
As long as the rest. Your good fellows who sing,
And who play, and make speeches, and do every thing
As if that were their *forte*, have the best of us noodles
Who count with the ladies about as their poodles, —
Poor curs, our one talent the meek one of following,
Led by a string. When I see women swallowing
Music like Trent's, with their hearts in their faces,
As ready to yield him their love and embraces
As even to listen and praise, I am vexed
That with dower so meagre I ever was sexed
With the males. It's discouraging, isn't it?"
         Waiting
No answer, not stayed by the half-hesitating
Appeal that spoke out of her face, he asserted:

"If ever coquettes have outrageously flirted
With men, it is men of his fortunate class.
The less charming ones they are content to let pass
In the main, as not worthy their wickedest wiles,
And we get what I call their superfluous smiles.
We are lucky, perhaps, after all, in not knowing
The sharpest effects of their skill, and in going
Unscathed where the cleverer fellows receive
Cruel injury."

    White to her lips, and in tones
That were trembling, and swift might have sunk into
  moans,
She besought revelation of mystery hinted
At thus in his words.

    " 'The Palladium' printed
A paragraph, saying your friends had been drowned."

" So I've heard. They were caught in a storm, and we
  found
Their boat empty and broken the following day,
After searching for hours. The quick journalist's way
Was to telegraph promptly their death. When they came
Back alive, as they did, they were rather to blame
For denying a fact: so the newspaper said
Nothing of it, and silently left them for dead."

The hard ring of his sentence sarcastic was much
Like a dash of cool water when fainting: its touch

Gave her strength. Yet her heart appeared swelling to
    burst,
And her lips were as dry as if parching with thirst;
And a great dizziness overcame her so nearly,
She whispered a prayer.
             "Percy Trent's case was clearly
A desperate one after that. So romantic
Conditions must plunge a man in the Atlantic
Of love beyond rescue. He fled from his fate
Like the coward all men are with flirts. I should hate
To be hit in the heart as he's been; for these poets
Take hard any hurt of that kind, though I know it's
Quick over with often. He'll write better verse
After this; and his life will not be any worse
For the blow she has dealt him."
                      "You think Mrs. Lee
Is unmerciful then?"
            "Yes. I know her to be
A coquette of the wickedest, once she attempts
Any conquest in earnest. She kindly exempts
From her efforts all average men, for they sicken
Her soon; but a man of some genius can quicken
The strongest allurements within her. She gives
Herself cheerfully over to winning him; lives
In the pleasure she finds in her growing success;
Leads him on in the quietest fashion, with less
Of apparent desire than indifference; wins
All his worship, and — stabs him."

"And wickedly sins
Against womanhood," warmly she answered him, throbbing
Her heart through her speech. "There can never be robbing
More wanton than takes of the treasure of life
For the taking, then presses keen Cruelty's knife
To the vitals, and leaves it."

"The stab never reaches
So deep as that quite, and the victim beseeches
A cure from some sister of mercy. The curate
Her ministry finishes. All must endure it, —
The wound and the treatment, I mean." And he sneered
In his cynical fashion.

She trembled, and feared
To reply.

"As for Trent," he continued, sarcastic
Yet earnest, "his love, I believe, is elastic
Enough to rebound from the bitterest strain.
He will weaken a while with the shock and the pain;
But in time he will marry that sister of mercy,
Who never may dream that the poems her Percy
Produces hereafter take color and tone
From a love that was earlier born than her own.
It's the way of the world. When with kisses we wed,
We have stood by the grave of some passion, and shed
The hot tears of forgetting."

"You speak for the men,
It may be;" and she rallied indignantly then.
"Men may love and forget: women love till they die."

"Then they stand at the altar, I fear, with a lie
On their lips many times," he responded. "The chances
Don't favor fulfilment of early romances.
We're creatures of fate, or of hard circumstances
That govern us, come between us and the kindest
Conditions of being, and lead in the blindest
Of paths. Women do with their love as they must;
And the truest of faith, the sublimest of trust,
Cannot yield the full fruitage of love absolutely
And ever. A woman may love when she mutely
Must look her farewell. If she never forgets,
She pays penalty twice, in her love and regrets,
For the sex that compels her to silence. She ought
To have recompense rare for a fact that is fraught
With unfairness the greatest, — the fact that avers
A man's freedom of speech, and then robs her of hers.
But suppose she were granted like freedom of voice,
It might chance that she make an unfortunate choice,
And win only refusal, and go disappointed
Away, as the men do, you know. It's disjointed
And cruel and wrong, if the woman must cling
To her love when it comes to be only a sting
And a weariness to her."

He spoke with a ban
On his flippant expression, that frequently ran
To severity reckless. If ever sincere
And believing, he seemed to be now.
"You appear
Full of sympathy, major, for women who fail
To find sweetness in loving," she said; and her pale
Cheeks were glowing with color returned. "You would make
Of their love but a fancy short-lived, for the sake
Of in charity sparing them pain. You contend
That love blooms like an annual, ready to lend
Of its fragrance to him who will water it well
When its winter of grief has gone by. You compel
A belief that we love as we like, and our fancies
Are cherished or dropped as the fortunate chances
Of being direct. But I cannot accept
Such a theory. Granted that women have wept
Bitter tears, and then wiped them away, and then carried
A smile for their friends, — even say that they married,
And grew into matrons with faces like saints
For the happy light in them, and made no complaints
Of the past, — I believe they remembered, and knew
That they never could wholly forget, and were true
To the law of their natures. God made us to love;
And we love for a purpose beyond and above
The mere loving. Some discipline comes to us, up

From the dregs that are found in the bitterest cup,
That we never should learn, did we drink and forget."

She was smiling, with tears in her eyes, that she let
Slip away unawares down her beautiful cheeks;
And the major observed them.
                              " Who foolishly seeks
To convince any woman," he said, " must repent
And be silent, or soon be convinced. I'm content
To admit you the argument, since you appeal
To economies only your faith can reveal,
And my questioning doubts. Divine purposes blind
Me wherever I turn. Where they seem to you kind,
They appear to me cruel. One loves and is glad,
And another goes out from her paradise sad,
And in sorrow she ought to forget; and you say
She must always remember, for this is the way
That her Maker has ordered. He brings her, you think,
A deep draught the most bitter, and bids her to drink;
And she never may sweet enough happily sip
To remove the bad taste that is left on her lip.
It is better to drink and forget, as men do
Who sip kisses of comfort, devotedly woo
Where 'tis easy to win, and make matches at last
For the happy-faced matrons who cling to their past
Without evident grieving."
                          His words had the ring
Of fine irony in them.

"Some bitter draughts bring
Their own subsequent sweetness," she answered. "The
    taste
May grow pleasanter to us, though never effaced:
It may lose all its bitterness even, and leave
Little more than the kiss of a friend. We may grieve,
And be glad even while we remember; for God
Will be kind, I am sure, and will spare us the rod
Of a wretched remembrance when once we have learned
What his wisdom would teach. He has tenderly turned
Many Marahs to wells of refreshing and strength.
I believe every heart can find gladness at length
In the faith that all lessons of God are as good
As the Master himself."

                    "And no reasoning could
Be so strong as your faith," he replied. "I should
    know
It were idle to challenge that. Since I must go
Very soon, I'll admit I am vanquished."

                                    He laughed
In his easy and spirited way, and with craft
And with cunning address he diverted their speech
Into other relations; yet often the reach
Of his cynical comment was cruel and keen,
As with utterance sharp it went flashing between
A half-credence and ready denial. He spared
Nothing reverent now from allusion that dared
To be lightly irreverent, measured and mocked

GERALDINE.

The pretences of creed and profession, and talked
Like the doubter he was.
        Many heard him, and felt
A quick shrinking and pain from the blows that he dealt
Without mercy wherever he went; but the most
Only laughed at his wit and the half-hidden boast
In his words of a wise unbelief, and took pleasure
In hearing him. Gifted with insight to measure
The feelings that shyly kept silence, he sounded
The shallows of conscience and motive, and bounded
The average purpose with ready precision,
Then singled them out for sarcastic derision,
And sneered at their shame.
        When at length he had ended
His call, and, with delicate lightness intended
To soften his previous words, he had said
An adieu, the mixed feelings of Geraldine led
To as mingled expression. She wept, and she smiled
Amid weeping. She uttered her thanks, like a child
In return for a token surprising, to Him
Who had spared her belovèd. With eyes growing dim,
And with language that faltered, she prayed him to keep
Her belovèd as hers, that none other might creep
In between her warm heart and his own, that their ways
Might be never divided. She prayed, as he prays
For his soul who is losing it, pleading, with pain,
That she never might know the wild longing and vain
Of a love unrequited. She whispered the name

Of her lover in tenderness sweet (though it came
Through her tears) in the confidence always she gave
To her Lord, and besought him in mercy to save
Them from drifting apart. Yet her heart by and by,
In the midst of her need and her longing, could cry,
" Let it be as thou wilt, loving Father; for mine
Is the weakness of love, but the wisdom is thine."

XXI.

In the late summer's glory that softly suffused
All the world, Percy Trent idly, dreamily cruised
Down the River St. Lawrence. The wonderful sweep
Of its waters grew wider and grander. The sleep
Of the sunlight upon them, unstirred by a dream
Of wild passion, was sweetly unbroken. Supreme
In majestical beauty the river rolled far,
Through a land where the deepest of solitudes are,
On its widening course to the sea. In the mood
Of its marvellous peace, that serenely did brood
O'er the scene, he went sailing away to content.

When the afternoon lengthened, and day was far spent,
They caught sight of Cocouna, where wealthy Canadians
Saunter in summer like happy Arcadians.
Trim and white-visaged, it sat on the shore,
Miles remote from the steamer that steadily bore
For the Saguenay's mouth, far across; and it seemed
Like a city set low in the sky, as it gleamed
On the crystal horizon, — a city of cloud,
Far away from the din and the fret of the crowd,
In some country of silence.

At Tadousac's wharf
They made landing, and tarried to look at its dwarf
Of a church, and the relics of centuries dead.
Pretty Tadousac out of its stillness has said
Not a word for the foreigner's hearing. It hides
In its modesty shy where the Saguenay's tides
Pour their inkiness into the mightier flow
Of St. Lawrence; and none of its quiet can know,
And the charm of its solitude strange, till they stand
On the beautiful beach, where its delicate sand
Ever tempts the most delicate feet to a bath,
Or go straying alone by some vine-hidden path
To the bluffs overlooking the river and bay.
In the dark of the waters, white porpoises play,
And make merrily bright the tranquillity there;
But no music of birds is borne out on the air,
And no whirring of spindles, no clangor of steel,
And no screaming of whistles, make frequent appeal
To your sense of activity. Languor and rest
Are as opiates here; and the common behest
To a laborer's brain and his wearying heart,
To arise, and in duty and doing take part,
Is a whisper unheard, where the speech of the time
Is in whispers, with rest for its rhythm and its rhyme.

In the deeper and mellower hush of the night,
Amid shadows that shut the wide world out of sight,

They went sailing north-west. The next morning at seven
The Bay of Sweet Laughter, that looks up to heaven
Untroubled and glad, — sunny Ha-Ha, — gave greeting
With smiles of surprise. As the morning sped, fleeting
As mornings of pleasure and peace ever seem,
The sharp bow of the steamer was set down the stream,
And they sailed with the tide through the silence. A shell
Of pure pearl was the sky overhead, and it fell
In its purity silvern and white to the hills
On the left and the right. If the Lord ever stills
A fierce tempest of feeling run high in the breast,
With the might of his word to an infinite rest,
It is here. If the silence of God ever falls
In its tenderness down on the world from the walls
Of the City of Gold, they have known it who sailed
Through the Saguenay's stillness.

       No mariner hailed
Their approach, and no fisherman shouted his word
Of salute. The soft calm of the air never stirred
To harsh utterance here, or the wing of a bird
Flying wearily home to his nest-keeping mate.
From the bold, rocky heights that were grim, desolate,
And untenanted, bounding the river's deep black
From the sunny Ha-Ha to the quaint Tadousac,
Never came to their ears or their vision a sound

Or a signal the solitude deep and profound
To disturb.
    Cape Eternity, grandly uprearing
Its dome to the azure, invited their nearing,
And thrilled them with awe of its might so tremendous.
Cape Trinity, opposite, lifted stupendous
And mighty its masses of granite to greet
The sublimity facing it. Majesties meet
In no kinglier fashion than these, as they tower
Far into the deep of the blue in their power
Titanic, from out the deep blackness below;
And no gloomier depths in their sombreness flow
To the sea than the deeps of these desolate capes,
That in silent solemnity cover their shapes
Half the altitude marvellous. Sailing beside
Their huge granite upheavals, the pomp and the pride
Of humanity fade to forgetting, in awe
Of the Infinite Presence that never man saw
But on mountains majestic and lonely. The lift
Of their faces is Godward; and sudden and swift
Is the leap of our thought from each adamant crown
To the Spirit eternal that loving bends down
With a glad benediction forever.
      Too soon
Came the close of that sheeny and bright afternoon
As they sailed down the river of silence. The sweetest
And gladdest of days is forever the fleetest:
It slips into yesterday's arms, and we say

A good-night to its pleasure and peace in the gray
Of a twilight that will not forbear. If it take
Of our heart's-ease, and cruelly leave but the ache
Of disquietude, hunger, and longing, what need
That we wonder and grieve? They are blessèd indeed
Who their faces have steadily set from the past,
And who will not look back.
      The next morn they made fast
To the wharf at Quebec, and Trent hastened by rail
To the hills of New Hampshire. A summer day's sail
Has its charm for the soul in disquiet: the ills
Of unrest are forgot in the calm of the hills
Everlasting. Who walks where their grandeur uprears
Should be glad with a hallowing gladness that cheers
Like a word of the Lord never lost. In the strength
Of their masterful quiet and glory, at length
He should stand as do they, with their face to the throne
Of their Maker, in patience, and wait.
         As alone
Through the mountains he wandered uplifted, his soul
Catching glimpses beyond of the land of its goal,
He was near to content. He could muse, in a mood
Of serene exaltation, on passion that wooed
Him astray from the pathway of duty, nor shrink
From the wearisome way he must journey, nor think
Bitter things of himself. In this mood he could lie
On the sunniest slope, see the fleets of the sky
In their fleecy white silence float dreamily by,

See the thistledown drifting at peace on the air,
Hear the tinkle of bells far below him, and care
For no morrow of possible pain.
 Yet aware
Of the days that awaited, nor happily blind
To their certain unrest, though now calmly resigned
In a willingness patient, he staid to behold
The glad summer in garments of scarlet and gold
Proudly decking herself in the early September,
While sweetly she tarried in dreams to remember.
Ere leaving, the mountain-top highest he climbed,
And with vivid and sorrowful prophecy rhymed,
Out of vision unclouded, and quieted fears,
And pathetic concern, of

THE VALLEY OF TEARS.

If I climb to the mountains of gladness,
 And bask in the sunshine of bliss,
If unheeding all sorrow and sadness,
 Forgetting the good that I miss,
I look out from my uplands of being
 Across the broad reach of the years,
I grow tenderly sober at seeing
 The shadowy Valley of Tears.

It is never quite lost to my vision,
 Though often beyond it I see
The green slopes of the summits elysian
 That wait with their blessing for me;

And, though often I long for the freedom
   That yonder eternally reigns,
I remember that each has his Edom
   Before the glad Canaan he gains.

When my heart with tumultuous throbbing
   Takes up the sad burdens of men,
I go down amid sighing and sobbing,
   And walk the dim valley again:
A sober, sepulchral procession
   We make as we journey along,
With a grief for our only possession,
   A funeral dirge for our song.

There are willows above us low bending,
   That weep with us over our woe;
And the mist of the mountains, descending,
   Bedews all the way as we go.
In the dark of our dubious grieving
   We walk as if stars had gone out,
And our souls were grown sick of believing
   The morrow were more than a doubt.

There are hearts, with their hunger pathetic,
   That walk in the Valley of Tears;
There are souls, in their sadness ascetic,
   That linger and grieve through the years;
There are loves that come silently hither
   To seek for some treasure of cost,
And that mourn, as a bairn for its mither,
   The wonderful love that is lost.

There are many who wait and who wander
   Within the dim valley with me,

And who yearn for the mountain-tops yonder,
   The sunlight and gladness to see;
But a stranger I look in their faces,
   And strangers they look into mine;
And as strangers we grope for the places
   Where sunlight and gladness may shine.

For who walks in the valley so lonely
   Goes there in his sorrow alone;
And who gives friendly greeting gives only
   For bread to the hungry a stone.
They may touch us whose yesterdays tender
   Made loving and living supreme;
But our grieving refuses surrender,
   And friendship was only a dream.

I am far up the mountains of being:
   The mists of the morning below
In their beauty shut out from my seeing
   The valley where soon I must go;
But I know, though the sun of my hoping
   May shine with a gladness that cheers,
That I soon shall be wearily groping
   My way in the Valley of Tears.

You may smile on the summits of gladness
   Who never have wept at their base;
But in time with the garment of sadness
   You closely will cover your face;
And unknown of the many who wander,
   Unknowing as they are unknown,
You shall grope for the radiance yonder
   Across the dark valley alone.

Amid pitiful sobbing and sighing
  Where willows and cypresses bend,
You shall walk where the shadows are lying,
  And see not a sign of the end:
You shall know, by the twilight unbroken
  When morn on the mountain appears,
You have come, without warning or token,
  At length to the Valley of Tears.

XXII.

When she read the long letter of Percival Trent,
Loving Geraldine Hope of her tenderness lent
To its words, and they gladdened her. Still he was hers
In possession the truest.   No doubt ever stirs
The fond heart to keen throbbings of pain, but is stilled
By repeated assurance of love.   Never thrilled
Any love with the pang of distrust, but could glow
With the gladness of faith come again, like the flow
Of a tide that has ebbed.
                         But a striking omission
She saw by and by, that began to condition
Her happiness new.   Not a word had he penned
Of his late episode: from beginning to end
There was not an allusion, in fact, to his friend
Mrs. Lee. It was plain that he could not have known
Of the published report of their death that had flown
With such cruelty to her ; more bitterly certain
It seemed that his silence had drawn a thick curtain
Between her and part of his past. She resented
His action at first, and then swiftly repented
The feeling she had not expressed ; for he knew
What was best for them both, and in kindness he drew

GERALDINE.

Any veil that might hide her from seeing. Till he
Should the curtain uplift, she would reverent be,
Nor profane it with curious touch. She could wait,
In the patience of prodigal love, for the late
Revelation that love would compel. If it never
Were made, if by strange providence she must ever
Relinquish the love that could make it, perchance
In a clearer to-morrow the dark circumstance
Would light up into blessing. God knew.

           If she came
In the trust of her faith to a pitiful blame
Of her love, to a fear that so worthful and sweet
An incoming as this in her life were not meet
For the Master's approval, or, tearful, to ask
If he chose to place on her the pain-giving task
Of upyielding it, could she obedient lay
The dear sacrifice on the Lord's altar, and say,
"I have given thee, Lord, all the sweetest and best
That is mine"? — if the loss of her love, as a test
Of her love for the Master, came to her at length,
And she struggled and doubted and wept till the strength
Of her faith overpowered her heart, — be not swift
To assert that she lacked the great womanly gift
Of deep loving; and wait till all women you learn,
Ere you doubt if the heart of a woman can turn,
When the weakness and longing of love make it falter,
And give of its riches unspared on the altar
Of God.

There are heroines kneeling alone
In their Holy of holies, or sitting unknown
Where the multitudes worship, whose offerings, made
In the silence of faith seldom doubting, have paid
Dearer tribute than incense of patriarchs. Laid,
With the lingering touches of womanhood tender,
In tearful but cheerful and hallowed surrender
Before the veiled face of their Lord as he waited,
Such offerings precious and costly were fated
To pleasure him better than blood, and to win
Recognition as precious. They only begin
To approximate love, who in selfishness sin
By withholding its wonderful treasure and sweetness,
And hindering so the perfected completeness
Of full consecration.
                    And Geraldine felt
All the deepest assertion of love when she knelt
And said, "Lord, if this thing that to me is so dear
Has been wrong in thy sight, let me hallow it here
With my tears of upgiving, and yield it to thee
To do with as thou wilt." She could generous be
With the Master, not doling him meagrely out
Of her poverty's wicked withholding and doubt,
But as lavishly yielding her riches, and knowing
The best she could give must be beggarly showing
To God, the one Giver of all. Though she gave
With a liberal heart, that was noble and brave,
She well knew that the end was not won in her giving;

That sacrifice sweetest to God is a living
Obedience daily, when truly obeying
Is harder than praise, and more costly than praying.
She knew, if the Lord should her offering take,
She must make it complete through the lingering ache
Of her heart in the wearying days to be met;
That the Lord could not mean her to drink and forget,
If he gave her the cup.
      She was human; she rose
To no saint-nature, clad in angelic repose,
In this crisis of faith: and how strongly she kept
Her humanity weak could be seen as she wept
For the love she might lose. In the time intervening
Ere Percival Trent came again, the full meaning
Of painful expectancy blossomed, and bore
Bitter fruit in her life. Now, as never before,
She was wearied and troubled of soul. For the rest
Of content she could sobbingly pray; but its blest
Benediction should come as the Master bestowed.
Though she longed for the peace like a river that flowed,
She but caught an occasional draught from its brink,
As her thirsty soul pined, even panted, to drink
To its measureless blessing.
      When Trent came at last,
From her wearisome doubting and fearing she passed
To a loving acceptance of good in to-day.
She made glad, in her simple and beautiful way,
His return to her love. He was hers once again, —

The one prince of her heart mid the nobles of men.
She would trust till he told her to doubt; she would show
How she trusted and loved till he made her to know
He must fail of requital.   Perchance, if he cared
For another, her love, if it maidenly dared
To give new revelation of being, would lure
Him away from his fancy to faithfulness sure.
Could the Father forbid an endeavor so pure,
And deny it success?   Could the semblance of sin
Be in any beguiling made only to win
And to keep what she felt to be hers?   Worthy winning
It was; and the Father such dutiful sinning
Would quickly forgive.
      Do you wonder that Trent
For a time could believe the strong passion was spent
He had wrestled with so?   He had come from the hills,
With their peace fresh upon him, their masterful wills
Overmastering feverish impulse.   He came
Full of purposes faithful, and penitent shame
Of his former unfaith, to be loyal and true;
And he stood by her side, undeserving, he knew,
With no wish beyond happiness present, believing,
In blind, willing credence, that folly's sore grieving
Was ended.   She helped his belief with her sweet
Declarations unsyllabled.   Passion's defeat,
With the aid that she brought him, so timely and tender,
Yet strong, was complete, or so seemed.   Its surrender
He smiled at in strength over-rated.

They talked
In the language of lovers ; as lovers they walked
Where the waters run seaward by Rivermet's side,
To behold the tall maples in radiance dyed
Like the robes of a qeeen ; and, if peace were denied
In superlative measure, these twain, who received
Of its blessing more moderate, fondly believed
It enough.
When some good we have craved appears less
Than will meet our desire, we are prone to possess
The full bounty in easy imaginings, cheating
Ourselves that we may not be cheated, repeating
The pretty delusion, and letting it seem
To be fact: so we make of our moments supreme
A half-fiction, the truth very deftly disguising
That great expectation may be most surprising
In lack of fulfilment. Poor dolts that we are
Thus to carry our covetous folly so far !

XXIII.

In November, Trent lectured at L——. Mrs. Lee
Was again the one hearer responsive to see,
Of all present, in scanning the crowd at the Hall.
He was moved by the current magnetic, and all
The quick feeling begot by a look in her face.
They who listened were stirred by the magical grace
Of his speech, as he never had stirred them before.
In the musical ring of his words there was more
Of a sympathy deep than he knew, or than those
Whom it thrilled could define or describe.
        At the close
Of his lecture she came to him, — came as the rest,
Who with greeting and compliment's flattery pressed
To his side; and they met in the casual way
Of a common acquaintance, with courteous play
Of inquiry and answer. The major took part
In their meeting, and studied them both with the art
He had mastered so well; but no secret he read
Of their innermost holding. Their manner but said
They were friends without interest deeper.
          They went
From the Hall as together they gossiped; and Trent

In her company supped, with the major. If either
Was thrilled by the strongest remembrances, neither
Gave sign. Conversation was easy, and ranged
From the grave to the gay at its will. They exchanged
Merry trifles of wit in the merriest fashion;
And none could have guessed that a powerful passion
Hid under such trivial speech and composure
So perfect. In vain for some look of disclosure,
Some word of deep meaning, the major made scrutiny
Keenest. Swift passion was dead, or its mutiny
Conquered by resolute will.
      And yet, leaving
To seek his hotel, in a partial deceiving
Of self as to feeling aroused, and believing
Too much in his strength to make safe his belief in it,
Percival Trent was unhappy. The grief in it,
Subtle, deep-seated, and dimly defined
As a grief, with a robbery keenly unkind,
Took away from his evening's endeavor the glad
Sense of triumph. He walked the still streets with a sad
Recognition slow forcing itself on his soul,
That the glamour of public approval is dole
But the poorest for peace of the heart.
       The next morning,
Regardless of silent yet forcible warning
Against it, he called on his friend; and she met him
With charming serenity graceful that set him

To wondering. Could it be she whom he heard,
When her feeling had swift every syllable stirred
With deep fervor, confessing a love too supreme
For denial, or silence, or death? Did he dream
She had lain on his breast, with her heart to his own,
In a bliss of possession too sensitive grown
To be painless? Was this the same woman who spoke
Of her wilderness barren and lonely, and woke
His quick passion's response? Was her winning repose
Like a calm of the tropics deceptive, that glows
With the heat underneath it to hurricane wild?

She received him with beautiful grace, that beguiled
Him anew. The warm grasp of her lingering hand
Within his, like a breath upon dark embers, fanned
His swift feeling to flame; but he struggled to hold
As serene a demeanor as hers, and controlled
Himself well. Without blushes, or faintest betraying
Of passionate force that was meetly delaying
Assertion, she talked like a woman long wed
With content, far removed from the girl who has said
Her first loving confessional. Part of the harm
She might do to a heart was hid under the charm
So elusive, that spoke of conditions beyond
Idle feminine art, or superfluous fond
Demonstration. His lecture she praised with a keen
Apprehension of meanings and truths; and between

Her sweet flatteries gave with a friendly temerity
Critical words that declared her sincerity,
Making the light of her praise appear strong
By the shade of her delicate frankness. As long
As it pleased her, they talked of the commoner things
Of experience, shunning the sensitive springs
That can open the heart; or discoursed of the newest
Attemptings in prose and in verse, and the truest
Successes of those who had won. She appealed
To the poesy in him expression to yield
With the power and art he might master, and give
Out of gifts that were his a few poems to live,
And win laurels undying.
                         " I honor the gifts
Of the poet," he said; " and my pen never lifts
To do rhythmic endeavor, but keenly it longs
For the genius to make it a singer of songs
That may gladden the future. The cruelest dower
Men have, I believe, is the semblance of power
They know to be weakness. We narrowly miss
A great good, and forever we fancy that this
Is the sum of our cruel defrauding. I hear
Now and then the sweet accents of Poesy clear,
And I strive to repeat them; but swiftly they fade
Out of memory. Silence her finger has laid
On my lips; and I feel, through the pain that has come
To my soul, it were happier far to be dumb."

"But the singers to whom the world listens must feel
The same bitterness often. They rarely reveal
The full music that thrills them: they breathe a few
　　　notes,
And the rest never hallow their fortunate throats
For our blessing. Moreover, no true singer's art
Was born in him whole statured. He learns of his heart,
And he sings as he learns. He must grow to the measure
Of full-singing strength in a studious leisure
Improved by the lessons of pain. You can turn
To the poet's best pages at will, and there learn
How he grew to his manhood poetic by reading
Between his own lines; for his silence makes pleading
Of sympathy. Do not you feel he has striven
To teach you in song what to him has been given
In cryings for utterance?"
　　　　　　　　　　Looking with furtive,
Quick glance in her face, he beheld the assertive
Appeal that so haunted it often, swift showing
Itself through her smile. With his blood quicker flowing,
Yet calmly, he spoke, —

　　　　　　　　"I suspect that you read
With a vision much deeper than mine; that I need
My poetic first lessons to learn now of you:
For no singer is heard without sympathy true,
And deep insight to see what are mysteries hidden
From all but the few. I believe you were bidden
To sing, and are wickedly silent. For me

There is only an echo of song: there can be
No outringing of marvellous notes that are mine
As I catch them direct from the singer divine
To whom poets all listen. And yet a refrain
May be tenderly sung till it softens the pain
In some sorrowing heart, and uplifts it. I'd ask
For no mission diviner, no holier task,
Were I laureate crowned for the world, than to sing
Of its sunshine, and on my strong melody bring
It forth out of the dark."

"By and by you will print
The best songs you have sung, and will give us a hint
Of the sweeter to come: I believe in your gift
As diviner indeed than you think. It should lift
You above the great chorus, who sing out of tune,
And torment us. You'll give us a tenderer rune
Than the many could breathe, if they stood at the door
Of the innermost temple, and listened, before
They began to make echoes of song. It will know
Sweeter cadence and mellower grace for the flow
Of last summer's experience into your being.
Some deeps of clear vision have come to your seeing,
You needed, for charity's sake and for love's,
To behold."

"I remember, my friend, that the dove's
Divine errand came after the storm. But, if sent
When the floods of this passion so idle are spent,
Will the dear dove of song, flying over the waste

Of my life, come again in her comforting haste,
Bringing olive-leaves?"
      She with her sudden allusion
Unmanned him; and he in as sudden confusion
Responded, he hardly knew how. With the look
That she gave him, his strong resolution forsook
Him, and fled. In its hunger pathetic he saw
The great want that would scorn to derision all law
Of denial, if free from its bondage of chains.
And that bondage — what was it?
      " For you there remains
Worthy work in the world, and who labors receives
In due time of his wages. Your dove's olive-leaves
Will bring promise of happy fulfilment to make
Your life rich with glad increase. You'll sing for the
  sake
Of the multitudes eagerly listening, and find
Your own gladness in service of song that is kind
Most of all to yourself. Good Samaritan singers
Are few, I believe, who divinely are bringers
Of oil and of wine to the wounded and sore,
And who fail of a blessing themselves as they pour
The sweet blessing on others."
      She spoke with some feeling,
Her words seeming tenderer still, as appealing
She looked in his face.
      " Could I sing you to peace,
I would stop by the wayside forever, nor cease

In my service of song till you bade me," he said
In his passionate utterance low.
       "But instead
You must sing for the mass," she replied. "I shall listen
More eager than they. In my heart I shall christen
As mine all the sweetest and tenderest things
You may breathe. I shall comforted say, ' Now he sings
For the neediest one, — for the one in the world
Who can take the rich treasure of sweetness impearled
In his notes, and feel gladdest and richest possessing it.'
Give as you may to the multitude, blessing it
Freely with giving's extravagant hand,
I shall count you my singer henceforth, though you stand
On the highest Parnassus, and I, sitting far
In the valley below, see you shine like a star."

With a mighty endeavor he mastered the tide
That was sweeping him on to expression denied,
Yet invited. He rose to depart.
       "I shall climb
To no height above yours; and my tenderest rhyme
Must forever fall short of the ministry sweet
I would lend it for you. Never song so complete
By a poet was sung as my longing desire
Would make vocal, if only these lips knew the fire
That is burning my heart. But my lips are as weak
As the lips of a woman."

He smiled.

"If, to speak
Of her love, a weak woman — the weakest — might dare
In the words that were fittest, you'd own that a share
Of the strength of her heart had been suddenly lent
To her lips." And the look that she gave to him sent
The warm blood to his breast. "And her lips need be
    strong
To repress what in utterance could be but wrong.
Do you doubt it?"

"Their silence is cruel, when speech
Would be cruelty worse. Let them tenderly teach
The same silence to mine." And he kissed her, repenting
At once the request and her ready assenting.

"Good-by! You will sing for me often," she urged.

The wild passion he wrestled with rioted, surged,
Through his heart. With a masterful effort he turned
To the door.

"When the singer's true art I have learned,
You may hear me. Good-by!"

He went hastily out
Of her presence, and into a torment of doubt.

XXIV.

But a day or two later a brief letter came,
Without prefix of date, or appendix of name;
And as Percival Trent read it, flushing and eager,
The forces of passion combined to beleaguer
His soul.
   "You have been here," the letter began:
"You have come and have gone. If our hearts overran
The hard limits we set for them, flowing together
Like parallel rivers in storm-laden weather,
Are we to be blamed? O my poet! the touch
Of your lips lingers yet upon mine; and, if much
Of my feverish longing and pain they reveal,
You who wooed them to speech must as gently conceal
Your displeasure. I never can bid you be dumb
Any more; for it seems to me now that the sum
Of my pain is your silence. I long so to hear
The dear words you ought never to speak, that I fear
I am foolish, unwomanly grown; and I crave
For the freedom to echo those words, as a slave
Must pine after the freedom forever denied.
As I see you far over the gulf yawning wide
And unending between us, I reach out my hands

And I call to you. Fate with its cruel commands
Would compel me to cease; but I cannot. I cry
Through the desolate distance, and say, 'By and by
He will hear me and answer.' You make no reply,
And my hope like a willow droops downward, and weeps.
I am learning the infinite pity that sleeps
In the bosom of God, I so pity myself.
As I count up the goods that I have, they are pelf
But the poorest compared with the treasure I covet.
I see it just out of my reach; and I love it
So wildly, and long with such longing to hold
It supremely my own, that my heart, over-bold,
Would compel the possession at once — if it could.

"O my friend! you who hold by the true and the good
With so steady a hand, you must come to my need
With your certain uplifting. I hunger, with greed
That can brook no denial, for life that is strong
In the truth, and that steadily sets against wrong
The unchangeable features of duty. You only
Can lead me up out of this solitude lonely
In which now I wait, by temptation beset.
When I stronger am grown, I may cease to regret,
And may go, with a face that is calm and determined,
Along the hard road where they march who are ermined
Of soul like yourself; but to-day not the weakest
Of women, among the most timid and meekest,
Is weaker than I. May Heaven pity me! None

Are so feebly outstretching their hands to the sun,
While they sit in the shadows, and shiver. The whole
Of my being is but a complaint. In my soul
There are only wild throbbings rebellious, and great
Sobs of pain, and these loud cryings-out against fate."

He was stirred to the deep of his nature, and wrote
An impulsive reply: —
      " To your passionate note
My heart beats a response that the flow of my pen
Can but coldly interpret. I kiss you again,
That my heart, overrunning my lips, may betray
To your own, throbbing fervidly under, what they
Could not fitly reveal, though endowed with the spirit
Of love pentecostal. They only who hear it,
Or feel it, know all the sweet emphasis hid
In love's tender, unsyllabled speech. If you bid
Me to breathe out a full revelation, I never
Can do it in words: I must make the endeavor
In language with meaning far deeper.
       " My friend,
I can lead you in worthiest way to an end
That is worthiest, only as steady I face
My hard duty apart from your side. In the grace
Of your presence 'twere easy to turn from the heights
I must climb, and to find in the sunny delights
Of my longing the gladness I crave. I could flee
From the path I must follow, and hold you to me

In possession defiant of duty, defiant
Of all your denial, supremely reliant
On need, — on your need and my own. To resist
The pathetic appeal of those lips I have kissed,
Till our souls came together; to hearken, and hear
Them beseeching my help in a cry that is clear
As the signal of love is forever, and stay
In the distance — ah! this is the trial that may
Overmaster my manhood, my being, at length.
If I ever can reach you my hands in the strength
Of uplifting to serve, and not sacrifice each
With its weakness, not long will you wait, and be-
  seech
For the aid I can render. I pity your need
With a pity unbounded, that can but proceed
From a love that is boundless. I hear the appeals
Of your heart with a throb of my soul that reveals
The deep pain I must suffer, the yearnings intense,
And the buffetings cruel. My way is as dense
With perplexities now as your wilderness long
Has been lonely and sorrowful; in it the song
Of sweet faith has died out into silence. Too stoutly
Distrust of myself is asserted, devoutly
To let me from self turn away to the might
That is certain. I dare not kneel down, and invite
For us both the one help that alone can avail,
When I know my petition must falter and fail
On account of so feeble desire. For confess

It I will: I would rather this moment possess
The great love that you give me, and know it my
    own
Undenying, in fullest of plenitude shown,
Than to pray you may learn its withholding, or learn
What is easier far, — to forget. And they burn
In my bosom, these words that might hint of return
I would make, as I do and I must; while my prayer
For denial of speech would go out on the air
With a wish that itself be denied, and my plea
For the strength to forget would but mockery be
Of too cherished remembrances.
                              "No: on the reed
Of my resolute purpose I lean, till to plead
For a better support I may dare, feeling true
To the want I shall syllable, pulsating through
My petition a longing sincere. Very tender
Indeed to the soul that in perfect surrender
Of wish and of will comes to him, are the greetings
Of God; but he never can hush the wild beatings
Within a poor heart that denyingly holds
To its pain. All my love your strong feeling infolds;
And as vain as I know it, as wicked as vain,
And as certain of sorrow, so sweet is the pain,
That I welcome it. Held in its clinging embraces,
We two may clasp hands, and touch hearts, though the
    spaces
Of infinite distance are rolling between."

While he still on the reed of his purpose would lean,
She made answer to answer of his : —

       " That you came
When I called you, can never be set to your blame,
Since you thought your response a denial instead.
To my hunger and longing you tenderly said
The sweet words that were manna to me; and they fed
When I famished. What need had my poor heart to hear
Your profession of love? I believe that the ear
Of cold Venus de Medici yonder would glow
Into rose, would you once for the marble let flow
Your warm current of masterful, passionate speech.
There is only one utterance now that can reach,
To revive it, this poor fainting soul that is mine, —
The assurance that still you do love me. Some sign
I must have, in my need, of that love, or I die.
You will grant it hereafter as quick, when I cry
To you over the deeps?

      " My belovèd, I try
To be patient and silent and brave. I would add
Not a pang to your struggle, nor sigh to your sad
But heroic endeavor. Instead, I would make
A glad martyr to-day of myself for your sake,
If I only could bring you content. For I love
You. So simple a thing to declare, but, above
All assertion, so forceful and sweet! The mild passion

Of maidens at school in as eloquent fashion
Might syllables take; but this love that I feel
Is as truer than that as the ring of white steel
Is more vibrant than lead. 'Tis a passion grown stronger
And deeper, and richer and sweeter, the longer
It slumbered: awakened, it holds me, and sways
Me at will. In the glow of those glad summer days
When it thrilled me at first, I half fancied 'twould seem,
When we parted, as only a midsummer dream:
In this sombre November the warmth of its flushes
I feel, as the maiden can feel her first blushes
At flattery paid; and so warmly it gladdens me
Now with its color and life, that it saddens me
Even to tears.

"Foolish tears! As they fall
Down my face, I am glad that hereafter not all
Of my bitterest weeping can rob it of sweetness
Your kisses have left; and my very unmeetness
For holy caresses so tender and pure
Can but make them in sanctified blessing endure.
O my friend! my belovèd! so close have I been
To the worst in the world, that the shadow of sin
Hovers grimly about me to frighten and grieve me.
Not mine was the fault; and, my darling, believe me,
The sin was no sin of intent, if to some
Like a sin it appeared.

"By and by you will come
To my love and my need, as it seems to you best,

With your love and your plenty. You cannot have
    guessed
From these hints, my heart's heart, how I hunger and
    long
For your comforting presence and cheer, or how strong
Is the love I have weakly declared. With your face
Looking into my own, and your loving embrace
Giving courage and strength, I could better translate
A brief page of love's living epistle. Sweet fate
That will bring me some blessedest glimpses of you!
For I love you! And this is my only adieu.''

XXV.

EARLY winter went by. It was fortunate, truly,
That Trent was so much in demand; for unruly,
Impulsive desire must have led him astray
From his purpose so true, but for need to obey
The imperative calls of the public. By night
He would speak to the crowds; and by day he would write
For still wider persuasion in print. Had they known
Who so eagerly heard him, how often a moan
Of disquiet was hid by the utterance strong
That so quieted them, or how frequent the wrong
He was fighting within bore him down, while he wielded
His blows on the wrong from without, they'd have yielded
Their sympathy freely as yielding their praise.
There were hours when he rose like a victor, and days
When he sank in the dust of defeat. There were seasons
When Duty made plain all her eloquent reasons
For holding him firm to his wearying course;
There were times when his passion took terrible force,
And so bitterly pressed him, so sharply assailed him,
That faith in its feebleness faltered and failed him,
And night swept him into its pitiless gloom.

It may be he was morbid by nature. The bloom
Of all beautiful things, it is certain, bore fruit
In his thought; and he wisely and kindly was mute,
If but ashes of apples he frequently tasted
Instead, or but seldom unhappily hasted
To tell of their bitterness.
                              Men are too free
With complaining recitals. Far better 'twould be
For us all, if the troubles that fret and annoy
Were but hidden away in a privacy coy,
And not prated about to our fellows. Far better
To make them for sunshiny gladness our debtor,
Than beg of their sympathy often, and take
Of its costly bestowal at will, when the ache
Of their life may be deeper than ours. If we urge
Our own woe on their ears, and go wailing a dirge
Over happiness fled, we shall hear enough minor
From them and ourselves to forget all the finer
And happier music of hearts.   .
                              When he went
For another day's tarry at Rivermet, Trent
Was subdued in demeanor, and notably carried
Himself with restraint; but he partially parried
His Geraldine's questioning look. He was weaker
Than wont, he explained. The hard strain on a speaker
Had worn him uncommonly. Seldom he slept
Until nigh to the morning. His labor had kept
Him from adequate rest through the day; he had used

Of his vital resources too freely, abused
The great blessing of health, and must pay for it dear
In depression and dulness.
      She gave him the cheer
Of her outflowing love, though it seemed to her heart
An impassable wall had arisen to part
Them still further. She knew by some keen intuition,
That once he would come on his lover's glad mission
Of love with a happier feeling, and say
Sweeter words than she now must expect. And the day
For distrusting might come to her soon! With the
  dread
Of its darkness upon her, she faintingly fled
To her Father, and unto his pity she cried
For the strength she would need.
      When she, troubled, replied
To the honest complaining of Trent, though evasive
As honest, she urged him with feeling persuasive
To seek a long rest amid scenes that were new.

"Put an ocean of green, or an ocean of blue,
Between work and yourself," she suggested. "Go over
The billowy prairies, or turn again rover
By sea, and get hearty and happy and strong."

"But the time of my absence might seem to you
  long;
And next summer, remember, we were to be wed."

"So you planned it, I know," hesitating she said;
"But it may be God means us to wait. I have prayed
That our marriage may be in some manner delayed,
If for any good reason it should not take place
As we fixed." And the serious look on her face
Told how earnest she was. "When the winter is ended,
The wealth of your life will have been so expended,
You'll need a whole summer of rest to regain
The great loss. Go away. If it seem to be plain
When the late summer comes, that our wedding should
wait
But your presence, no distance can be to you great
That you journey on errand so glad;" blushing now
At her words, as she uttered them shyly.
"I bow
To your bitter decree," he responded, not daring
To trust a more serious answer. "The faring
Of bold pioneers in the West has invited
The vagabond in me since youth. I have slighted
The call every year: now I'll heed it, and go
To the region of sunset so soon as the snow
Shall have vanished. But trust me to come to you soon
When you freely will give me the coveted boon
Of yourself."
"And I freely will do it when truly
It seems to be best; yet I would not unduly
Make haste. We must try to be certain, and take
Every step as the Master may lovingly make

The way clear. He will show us his path for our feet
If we ask him."
"Your faith is as certain and sweet
As my own is uncertain and vapid too often.
'Twould light up the gloomiest way, and would soften
The hardest and ruggedest path. Do you never
Have doubts of the Master?—of all your endeavor
To touch him for healing of soul, when you press
To his side in despair of aught else?"
"I were less
A weak woman, and more like a saint, could I hold
To my faith without doubting forever. As bold
As was Peter, he sank in the wave when he walked
To his Lord; and my weakness has bitterly mocked
Me at times when I should have been strong. We must
    doubt,
I suppose, being human; and heartsick, without
Any help of ourselves, we too often must stem
The thick crowd of our doubts and our fears, ere the hem
Of the Healer's soft garment we touch."
"And you feel
That the Master walks always near by, and will heal,
If you press through the throng to his side? Though
    unseen,
You are sure he is there?"
"There are times when between
Him and me I can see only blackness; but still
I believe I shall find him through doing his will;

And he never is lost.   It is I who have strayed
From the way that he journeys.   I seek him, afraid,
Till I hear his quick question, 'Who touched me?' and then
I am glad."
Far less tender and reverent men
Would have thrilled to her thought and her tone sympathetic,
And smothered in silence all questions heretic
That might have been syllabled.
"Faith is magnetic
As love, when it speaks from a heart beating free
With the healthiest life ; and your faith upon me
Is electric.   I feel it more keenly, indeed,
Than I feel my own faith from within.   When my need
Is the greatest, I wonder if once I believed,
Or made pretence of trust."
She was troubled and grieved
At his words.
"You are living, it may be, too mainly
In self, are depending too much and too vainly
On strength of your own, to be sure of the way,
Or of light in the dark.   We must serve him to-day
With our might, when the strongest we feel, would we know
The Lord's help in our weakness.   The farther we go
Independent of him, in an idle belief
In ourselves, the more certain some brambles of grief

Will be found in our pathway to prick us, the more
Is it sure that our questions will trouble us sore.
It is easy to doubt," a quick thrill running through
Her brief words as she uttered them. "Men who, like you,
Are endowed with large manhood and generous life,
Have the amplest endowment for doubting. The strife
Of unfaith and belief must oft carry them far
From the face and the voice of the Master. They are
To be envied for strength, to be pitied for weakness.
Their manliness strong and assertive the meekness
Of faith overcomes ; and a faith that is proud
Of the manhood that holds it will some time be bowed
To the dust."

"If I ever have foolishly classed
My weak self with the strong, the brief season is passed,"
He responded half bitterly. "Few are so weak,
And so conscious of weakness, as I. But I seek
The great Fountain of strength without finding, and dwell
Weary days in a desert where flows but a well
Of deep bitterness ever, and drink till I thirst
As do they who are famishing utterly. Cursed
By the keenest of longings for peace and sweet quiet
Of soul, I am held where the tumult and riot
Are greatest, till often I sigh for the rest
Of that sleep never ending."

                    She trembled, and pressed
Back the tears that her sympathy quick could have shed.

"But you always are out of your desert-place led,
When at last you are willing to follow the leading
Of God, are you not? Our most pitiful pleading
Is vain, if we make it while wickedly clinging
To ways that we ought to forsake. The sweet bringing
Of peace to our souls is along the hard road
Of some duty we would not perform." And there
        glowed
In her face the glad light of a full consecration.

"Perhaps if we knew not some great desolation
Of God," he rejoined, "we should never feel sure
Of his fatherhood; and, if we cannot endure
To be fatherless so for a little, how could
We be orphaned forever? Believing is good
That will bring an occasional glimpse of his face,
To make certain he is. I am glad of the grace
Of my faith, that at times can believe so completely,
And yours that so seldom can doubt, as they sweetly
Make better my life."
                    "But your faith may be fervent
And certain as mine, if you go as the servant
Each day of a Master most loving, who cares
But to bless you in service," she said. Unawares
She was blending rebuke with her words of appeal;

Yet no chiding of hers could be harsh. "You must feel
In your trouble and doubt, that you have not in all
    things
Lent willing obedience. Out of the small things
Of selfish idolatry oftenest grow
The great forests of doubt, into which we may go,
Beyond sunlight and shadow, far into the night."

"But we always come out into morning and light?"

"You and I, let us hope." And she smiled rather sadly.
"Some souls there may be who go onward so madly
Intent on their own wicked wills, that they sink
In abysses we miss, and are lost. When I think
Of their pitiful madness, their longing distress
In the dark, I could weep; for the way that we press
Is a hard enough way at the best. You and I,
When it troubles us most, may find comforting nigh;
But these wayfaring souls, without help or a hope,
Can but wearily on in the wilderness grope
Till the end."
    So they talked of the holiest things
Of the heart. So he drank from the up-welling springs
Of her beautiful faith, till his spirit grew stronger.
He left her sweet patience at length, but no longer,
As to it he came, full of bitter unrest.
The old song of belief that had slept in his breast
Woke to music again in a strain that was finer

And sweeter than once for the tremulous minor
That thrilled it. Complaint with new blessedness
    sharing,
He soberly sang by the way of

WAYFARING.

The way is long, O Lord, that leads
To cooling springs and fragrant meads:
I weary of its weary length;
I lose all heart and hope and strength,
As here I halt my tired feet
And pray for rest so far, so sweet.

I thank thee for a halting-place
Made glad by thine own smiling face;
I thank thee that the dusty way
Thy footsteps knoweth day by day;
I thank thee that some path there be
From pain and care to peace and thee.

Its rugged steeps I would not mind,
If, daily climbing, I could find
Secure repose at day's decline
A little nearer thee and thine;
If always from the mountain-peaks
My faith could see the land it seeks.

But when through gloomy vales I go,
That no glad sunshine ever know;
When even thy dear presence seems
A far-off thing of doubt and dreams, —
Forgive me, Lord, if then I faint,
And murmur oft, and make complaint.

I know my times are in thy hand;
I long for light to understand
How thou canst for each pilgrim care,
How thou canst hear each pleading prayer,
How unto thee each soul is known
As if it walked the world alone.

And some time I may comprehend.
The way is long; but at its end
A clearer vision waits the sight.
In thy dear garden of delight,
Wayfaring done, let me abide
Where never falls an eventide.

XXVI.

It was later by less than a fortnight, that Trent
Gave a lecture one night in the village of Ghent.
He had firmly decided he would not again
Meet his friend, Mrs. Lee; but each purpose of men
Is uncertain of issue. One only of all
The great number of faces that crowded the hall
Was familiar, and that one — was hers. As he caught
Her first answering look, a brief moment he fought
With his passion for mastery; then with the art
Of his utterance quickly he moved every heart
To responses of sympathy.
      Who can define
What is eloquence? Is it some thought half divine
And all noble? Or is it the audible sign
Of some feeling within that is striving to leap
Into being of speech? Is true eloquence deep
As the orator's soul, and as deep as the hearer's
He touches? Indeed, is it true that he mirrors
Some innermost thought of our own, unexpressed
Hitherto, and unformed, when we feel in our breast
The pulsations of pleasure that syllables seek
Without finding? Is eloquence strength for the weak

In expression, and lips for the dumb, who may speak
Through the wonderful words of another?
                                        The lecture
Was over at last, and the ready conjecture
Of Trent became truth. Mrs. Lee was with friends
In the place on a visit.
                        " The time comprehends
A surprise the most happy for me in thus hearing
And meeting you now," she remarked ; and, appearing
Unmoved in demeanor as he did, she asked
Him to go with her friends to their home.
                                        If they masked
Every passionate feeling in plain commonplace ;
If he sat amid strangers, and looked in her face
As he looked into theirs, with the courteous grace
Of attentiveness only to speech that was clever
Or trite as it chanced, — it may be his endeavor
Was small ; for his passion was passive. He curbed
It so stoutly and well, that it little disturbed
His composure at present. To-morrow? What matter
Defeats yet to come, if to-day only flatter
With victory?
              Leaving them all in an hour,
With placid serenity passing for power
Over self, he went out to his solitude grim
With its weakness defiant of strength. When to him,
But a day or two later, this brief message came,
In his breast he could feel the fierce breathings of flame :

"O my friend! are we always and always like this
To go on? Is a touch of your hand, or a kiss
Of your lips, to be all I can ever have granted
Of you? *You* could banish the ghost that has haunted
Me long. *You* could lift me up into the sun
From these shivering shadows.

     "How much you have done
For me now I can never reveal. As your debtor
I ever must be, unless loving you better
Than even I dare to confess is a payment
Acceptable. Ah! when I sleep in the raiment
Of death, will they look in my face, comprehending
How long and how sorely I needed befriending
That God only gives through his image? — the soul
Of a man's loving nature, to guide and control
My weak waywardness? — love that should hold my be-
  havior
In line with its purity true, be my savior
From all that could touch me to hurt or assoil,
In a merciful tenderness pour the sweet oil
Of its gladness on life's troubled waters, infold
All my faults in its mantle of charity, hold
Me apart in its own blessed heaven?

      "I know,
Could you stand by me, darling, (God grant it be so!)
When at last I am but a white silence, you'd hear
A new message to *you* through the calm atmosphere
Round about me. My lips might not move; but as clear

As the clearest articulate speech they would tell
Of the hunger that starved me to death. And so
    well
Would you then comprehend all the longing and need
I had suffered, I think you would pitying plead
For the seal of that silence in mercy to break,
That I might not eternally want. For your sake,
My belovèd, to tenderest speech I would come,
Though the highest archangel might bid me be dumb;
Out of pitiful rest the white silence would rise,
And beguile you with kisses, and quiet the cries
Of your heart for the loss of my love, and the grave
Would in mercy release me to you.
                                    "But a slave
To the hardest taskmaster — to Life — should not think
How much kinder a master might Death be. I drink
Of the bitterest draughts every day, then I dip
My cup deep in the well of your love, and I sip
Till its sweetness has gladdened me. Always athirst
And an hungered I am. My one darling! the worst
Of the Magdalenes dare to come near to the Christ;
And her faith, that was loving the sweetest, sufficed
To redeem her from sin. If no virtue were mine
But to love you, I fancy that this would incline
The one Master to pity me. Wicked as one
Who has never been pardoned, or ne'er has begun
To be penitent, still I could love you no more,
Were I good as the angels of God."

As before,
When she called to him thus in her passionate speech,
He responded, as moved by it strongly.
"You teach
The deep meanings of words," he made answer. "You tell me
Of love far beyond my belief; you compel me
To marvel that such a great love can be given
To me. And for what? O my friend! I have striven
To solve the hard problem, have striven to still
The strong, masterful throbs of my heart; but the will
Is as weak as the reason. Why love should lay hold
Of my being with mastery cruel as bold,
Is as dark and as blind as the will to resist it
Is feeble. To-day I should hardly enlist it,
If help were at hand that could victory give
To my feeble resistance. To-day I would live
In this marvellous love and the blessing it brings me.

"The honeycomb shelters the bee that quick stings me.
I taste of the sweets of your love but to feel
The sharp pain that its riches of blessing conceal.
You can never be mine. We are parted as much
As if never I felt the soft lingering touch
Of your kisses, — are parted as certain and wide
As the east and the west. If you hungered and died
In my absence, I could not come close to your side
In the nearness of love's divine freedom to weep.

Were I sleeping to-day the unanswering sleep
Of the grave, you must stand in the distance, and say
But a tearless farewell.
      " I am going away
When the buds begin bursting. Your duty and mine
Both demand that I should. We must follow the line
Of our separate fates. What your duty may be
I can only imagine : my own is to me
As unyielding as God. It is holding me now
With its fingers of steel, and in calmness I bow —
Though in merely the fiction, the semblance, of loyalty,
Need not be said — to its rigorous royalty.
Still, while I walk in the way that it urges
Me on, I can feel the impetuous surges
Of passion within me responding to yours ;
I can longing look back on your face as it lures
My return. Set it steadily forward, nor let
It look backward to me with its haunting regret.
Let us walk the two ways that lead farther apart,
As if love were a lie, and we lived without heart.

" Am I bitter and cruel? Forgive me, and know
That I write out of burning unrest.
        " I shall go
To the West in a month, to find peace, if I can,
On its plains and its mountains. The rigorous ban
Of my duty forbids me to see you again
Before going. I think if the strongest of men

Were to stand at your side, with his purpose as true
To another as purpose that God ever knew,
He would falter, and love you, and linger — unless
You compelled him to leave. So in safety I press
The last passionate kiss on your beautiful face
But in fancy: I hold you to me through the space
That divides us, but dare not in parting come near;
And I speak idle words could your heart only hear
You would echo them back with such winningness, I
Should wait near you to listen forever. Good-by!"

She began her reply with the utterance strong
Of a passionate nature unmastered.
                                    "I long
For your presence and cheer with a longing that leaps
Every barrier now, and compels it; that keeps
You beside me wherever you go. I shall cling
To your hand, though you journey as far as the spring
Is from winter, and climb to the uttermost heights
Of the earth; for I hold as the crown of delights
In all good that is fruitage of love, the keen sense
Of a bodily presence in absence — the tense
That takes hold of my yesterday's doing and being,
And keeps it material still to my seeing
To-day. You made yesterday worth such a keeping
To me. When you entered my life, all its weeping
To smiles of thanksgiving and gladness was turned.
I have learned the true meaning of life: I have learned

The sublimest of charity. Out of the wild
Of my desert so dreary, your love has beguiled
Me to come ; but alas for the many who faint
On the blistering sands, and whose feeble complaint
Is not heard ! And alas for the souls that are lost,
Ere the desert so barren and burning is crossed !

"My belovèd ! you cannot take leave of me here.
If our paths run apart, you are always as near
As affection can bring you ; so near, that I share
In your nobleness, feel the uplift of the air
That you breathe, am made better and truer by you.
It were folly to bid you a mocking adieu
When I know you must stay by my side in the spirit,
If not in the flesh. And my soul needs you near it
So bitterly often ! So often it cries
For the aid you can render, and waits the replies
Of your heart with so weary a waiting, I think
It would kill me, if now you should utterly sink
From my sight into echoless silence.
       "And yet,
Though my face may look back with its haunting regret
That will haunt it forever, I see but a dim
And a shadow-like semblance or spectre of him
Whom so madly I love. The true self that I need
With such hunger of needing will swiftly recede
Out of reach. And I feel so defrauded ! The whole
Of my womanhood owns you its master. My soul,

Being cheated of you, like a slave in distress
Can but moan by the way, with no bounty to bless
It, and bring it again to the face of its lord.
Without you I am always and only the ward
Of tyrannical want, and my poverty begs
For some opiate cup I may drain to the dregs,
And forget the great wealth I have missed.

"Am I writing
Unreason? Demented, am I but inditing
Vagaries absurd, as the contrary feelings
Of love I express in this manner? Revealings
Thus opposite ought not, perhaps, to be made
The same moment.

"If wild I may be, I have weighed
The hard problem before us, with reason that held
Me above the great hunger of love, and compelled
Me to heed. You have work in the world, and I will
Not make doing it harder. To-day I would still
Every longing of mine, but to spare you a pang
Of disquiet. The hope and the faith that you sang
Ere you saw me must yet in your singing abide,
Or I shall not forget that I ought to have died
Before hearing and seeing you. O my heart's heart!
Let me feel your strong throbbing again ere we part;
Let it teach me the courage of faith and of hope,
As along in the desert I desolate grope.
You will pardon the prayer? I'm not practised at praying,

And chiefly, I fear, have the habit of saying
My prayers unto you.
     "'God be with you!' I say
Now to *him*. For *your* sake I can fervently pray,
If I may not or dare not look God in the face
For myself. And I pray that some heaven-sent grace
May bedew you with patience wherever you go.
We have tested life deep enough, darling, to know
That victorious living is better and truer
Than happiness. May you the battle endure
Like a victor, and win, if not happiness, peace!
And remember, belovèd, I never shall cease
To aspire for you, hope for you, love you, be proud
Of your many successes, as if in the crowd
Of the world I alone had the right. And who ought
To be prouder than I? In my future, the thought
That I once was your friend, though forgotten I be,
Will seem sweet as another's remembrance to me.
I would rather have had my brief portion of you
Than be held in possession most perfect and true,
For a lifetime, of all other men. I am weak
With the passionate gladness that flows to my cheek
As you kiss me farewell. I am faint with the pain
That is flooding my heart as I call you in vain
Through the widening distance. The mist in my eyes
Becomes heavy, and stifles my pitiful cries."

XXVII.

Trent was true to his purpose. He went to the West
Without stopping to see Mrs. Lee. To the test
Of her presence he would not, he dare not, again
Bring himself.
        And his leave-takings troubled him when
He saw Geraldine last. A great tenderness thrilled
Through her loving good-bys. He could easy have
 · willed
To remain with her now, and possess her without
Any waiting; for over him brooded a doubt
That he could not have set into speech, — an impression,
That, leaving her thus, he was putting possession
Beyond him forever. Her words of farewell
Were so solemnly tender and sweet, that they fell
Like a sad prophecy on his ears.
        He had penned
A long letter to Isabel, making amend
For refusing the cry of her heart, by replying
In echoes as passionate. Firmly denying
Himself the great gladness of holding her yet
Once again to his breast, his quick pen would not let
Him keep silent completely. It revelled in words

That to listening of love were as music of birds;
And it told as with tears of his frequent unrest,
Of the longing and fears that his being possessed.

You will say he was weak. Let it pass to his credit
That he had discerned the same truth, and had said it
With bitter reproaches of self. And, beside,
Let it temper your judgment that he had denied
A temptation the greatest, — to go to her, give
To the winds every promise and duty, and live
On her riches of love. He was weak, and he knew it:
His weakness had caused him too often to rue it,
To leave him in doubt. He was weak: so are all
Who believe in their strength; and the many who fall
Into folly and sin are the arrogant souls
Who stand censor to others.
      We go to the goals
Of our strong aspiration in weakness that trips us
Again and again. The hard fortune that whips us
With discipline's lashes has oftenest found
Opportunity swift when we fell to the ground
With our faces uplifted in scorn of the weak.
If we find the great blessing of strength, we must seek
For it humbly, believing our need to be sore.

If the hills of the East have a charm to restore
Balmy peace to the troubled of soul, the wide plains
Of the West are as richly endowed. He regains

The sweet quiet of being who goes to them faint
With long striving for victory; doubt and complaint
Become rest and rejoicing; the rigors that goaded
Him on melt away in the sunlight, so loaded
With burdens of glory it glows like the blazing
Of tropical heat; and eyes weary with gazing.
The roll and the sweep of their reaches are grand
As the ocean unbounded; the billows of land
Float away to horizons far lapping the sky;
And the magical breezes blow ardently by,
As if bearing rich argosies over the sea
To some haven of hope. If infinitude be
Ever laid before mortals for dim comprehending,
It hides in the plains and their reaches unending.

The saunterer's mission was Trent's. He fulfilled it
Religiously. Time was his own: if he killed it,
And buried it out of his sight, he was winning
The wager of life. And he thought it not sinning,
In search of his bodily good, and the peace
Of his spirit, to throw away care, and to cease
From all studious habits. He lived like the men
Whom he met by the way. He abandoned his pen
For his rifle; spent weeks as a hunter with those
Who made hunting a business; laid down at the close
Of each radiant day with his face to the stars;
And sleep opened for him the imprisoning bars
Of his being, and freed him to perfect content.

The glad winds of the West in their sport came and went
Where unsheltered he lay; and, as boldly they kissed him,
Their marvellous vigor flowed into his system,
And so he grew strong.   He was seldom in reach
Of the mails, and but seldom, therefore, did the speech
Of his friends come to gladden or sadden him. One
Wrote as little of love as if scarcely begun
To believe herself loving; the other withheld
Not a passionate word, and her passion compelled
His replies. But he wrote to his Geraldine merely
The messages born of a love that sincerely
Is guarded of duty,— such letters as most
Of men send to their wives when their love is a ghost
Of the thing it once was, and comes only in sight
As a matter of habit when rarely they write.

Did he love her? He questioned thus daily. In vain
Did he say to his heart that the answer was plain
In the question itself. "Love *may* doubt," he could hear
His heart reason. "The love that is surest may fear
For its very existence. Wild passion may hide
It from sight; but it will not so swiftly have died
As you think. It is modest. It sits in the shade
Of assertion unblushing, and trembles, afraid
For its life. But hot passion is bold as the day,
And it knows no rebuking, nor fears to betray
Itself ever and always."

He held by the love
He had pledged to be true to, before and above
The strong feeling that shadowed it, e'en though his lips
Were so dumb to expression while passion's eclipse
Hovered over. Nor once did he say to its face
That it could not be love; that it came to a place
Not divinely its own; that the heaven-guided guest
Had more recently come to abide in his breast,
And the early intruder must go. Never through
The long days was he thus to his pledges untrue,
If untrue in a deeper and wickeder sense
He confessed himself. Either in fact or pretence
He was loyal to love in the positive, though
The superlative tried him for treason.

          The glow
Of young summer grew fierce on the plains, and he took
His way thence to the mountains; there swift he forsook
All the commoner haunts for those places where only
The few ever come, and in solitude lonely
Communed with the grandeur around him. He rode
Up and down the green valleys; he made his abode
For the night where the night overtook him, and slept
With no tent overhead but the azure that swept
From one summit of gray to another; he mounted
Magnificent peaks, till in wonder he counted
Their neighbors magnificent, lifting afar
Their white crowns to the purple; in gorges that scar
The calm features of Nature like pitiless gashes

Some Titan has made with his terrible slashes,
He marvelled anew, till this life, growing small
Mid the greatnesses round, seemed to dwindle, and fall
Out of sight; and he moved but an atom in space
Overhung by the Infinite's glorious grace.

In the grand exaltation of spirit that came
To him here, life had never a worthier aim
Than *to be*. Nothing grander than being can seem,
Where the mountains lift upward, majestic, supreme,
And eternal. They stand like old statues of time,
Looking God in the face. With the world in its prime,
They are hoary of head; and they gleam in the noons,
Turn to crimson in sunsets, and gray in the moon's
Mellow glory, as through the long ages asleep.
As the shadows of darkness fast over them sweep
When the moon is away, they grow ghostly and grim,
Till their majesties fade into distances dim,
And the hush of their silence is solemn as death.
When the dawn is at hand, its first crimsoning breath
Floats across the long reach of their summits to crown
    them
With colors of life; the dark shadows slip down them,
And seek the defiles where they lurk through the day;
Clear and strong their dim outlines come forth from the
    gray
Of the morning; and through the baptistical rays
Of the sun all their silence is priestly with praise.

XXVIII.

When the midsummer heat to its uttermost burned,
From his wild mountaineering alone Trent returned
To a town of the mines, for some letters expected.
On reaching the place he grew strangely dejected
In spirit, and felt a foreboding of ill
That he could not shake off, though he bent all his will
To the task.   It was time for his summons from her
He had promised to wed. If he went, should he err
Against both, to give vows before God to be true
Ere his passion was dead, and when truly he knew
It must face him with mockery? Should he not sin
Against God and his soul, were he soon to begin
Wedded life, while a woman he never might wed
Could so burden his peace with the words that she
      said?
Were it not the clear wisdom for him to postpone
Consummation distrusted till doubt should have flown,
And till love in sweet certainty came to its own?
In this questioning mood, there was put in his hand
A small package of letters, that quickly he scanned
For the two he cared chiefly to read; and he broke

Mrs. Lee's first of all. It was passionful; spoke,
In the phrases she forcibly used, of her feeling
Intense; called upon him anew for his healing
The hurt, "the sweet hurt of this sorrowful love,"
(That had grown in her being beyond and above
All beside, making other loves seem but the sign
Of weak tolerance now,) with the oil and the wine
Of his love-bearing speech: it, in short, was a letter
Of credit drawn on him at sight, as a debtor
To love, without limit, and paid by his passion
In throbs of response.
     With a face growing ashen,
When once he had fairly begun to peruse
The long letter of Geraldine, this was the news
That he read of her final decision, the sum
Of her reasons for failing to say he should come:

"MY DEAR FRIEND, —
    "Turn your face to the shadow a while.
You may make believe then, that I say with a smile
What the tears give me trouble to write. I am sure
That God bids me speak, or I could not endure
The hard duty.
    "I love you: let this be as plain
As I ever have made it to you, and remain
A fixed thing in your memory; though to refrain
From the simple confession were wiser, perhaps.
I shall love you, I think, till eternity laps

Upon time. It is sweet just to say it once more
While the right is still left me.
                              " You loved me before
You had come to the measure of love in degree
That is highest. You loved me as much as in me
Was the power to call out your deepest expression
Of love. I believe it, and hold the possession
Of that which was mine, and which may be mine yet,
Above rubies.
                    " But, though I may weep with regret
That I could not the deeps of your nature so stir
As another has done, I no longer demur
Against fortune that proved me so weak to excite
Your strong feeling, and showed you the higher de-
      light
That I could not awaken. And blame cannot live
In my heart against you. I have nought to forgive
Of unfaith: you have been to your pledges as true
As true purpose could hold you. A greater love grew
In your breast, and it would not be stifled.
                                        " I knew
Months ago of the struggle that wearied you, saw
How you battled in secret to conquer a law
Of your nature, and feared the defeat that impended.
You're battling to-day: but the fight will have ended
When this you have read; for I claim you no longer
As mine. You may yield to the love that is stronger
Than love given me, and be free to win much

As may answer to yours. And God grant that it touch
You to peace!
    "I have struggled to say this so long;
For I could not at first give you up. May the wrong
Of my selfishness find its quick pardon! I hoped
That my love might still hold you to me : but I groped
In a path growing dark, for my will was arrayed
Against God's ; and my wishes were most, I'm afraid,
For my happiness rather than yours.
      "You will make
No reply to this letter, but spare me the ache
Of repeating the prayerful decision contained
In it here. If you knew how my heart had complained
To itself, — how with ready excuses it plied me,
And long all the comfort of trusting denied me, —
You could be but pitiful now, as you must.
I have faith in your manhood and mercy : I trust
In your silence to help me do right. For the way
Opens clear to my sight ; and you never must say
To yourself or to me that you ought to fulfil
The faith plighted between us. I know that the will
Of the Lord is against it. I know that he tells us
To separate now ; and he always compels us
To hear him.
    "You must not feel blame because I
Make a sacrifice costly to me. By and by
Compensation will come to my soul for the loss
To my heart. By and by, shining sweetly across

The hard path that I go, I shall see the dear smile
Of my Master; and that will the way so beguile,
I shall cease to regret.

     "Do not think of me, then,
As unhappy forever, or urge me again,
Out of pity and honor mistaken, to wed you.
The love that against your own will has thus led you
Apart from me quite, was permitted for some
Divine purpose. I beg you, my friend, to be dumb
While I study the lesson that to me is taught:
When I fully have mastered it, life will have caught
A deep meaning but now only dimly defined,
And the Teacher will prove that his wisdom was kind.

"On a day that is distant, perhaps, we may stand
Face to face in a friendship with strength to command
Every thought of the past into silence and sleep.
Until then you will see me no more, lest I reap
Greater harvest of pain than to-day I must glean.
May God bless you in love and in life! May you lean
On his bosom for rest when you weary! May being
Grow broader and richer henceforth to your seeing,
And fill itself nobly with duties well done!
God be with you, and keep you!

     . . . "At last I have won
The long conflict. Henceforth I shall think of you
  mainly
As one who was dear, and is dead; and, if vainly

I seek thus to put you away, I shall know
That the Master would teach me still further, and go
Through the ways of remembrance till he leads me far
Where the pools of his peace and his blessedness are.

"Let me kiss you farewell, as a sister might kiss you
Who felt that for years she must want you and miss you.
Forgive the hot tears that will fall on your face.
I am heart-worn and weak; but the pitying grace
Of our Father will strengthen me. Into your eyes
Let me look once again, while the saddest good-bys
That I ever have wept trickle over my cheeks,
And my love its last picture for memory seeks.
Breathe a prayer with me now that not always between
The dear picture and me shall be tears.
                              "GERALDINE."

As he read and re-read it, quick flushes of shame
Brought the color anew to his cheeks, and swift blame
Of himself fell upon him. He saw, as by clear
Revelation, how weak he would always appear
In her sight, and how wickedly love had been wronged.
And he felt, that, in losing what once had belonged
To him wholly, he lost a great treasure of worth
Beyond any conception before.
                         The wide earth
Was between them. He knew her too well to assail
Her decision by reason or wish. To avail

Against faith like her own, against purpose so strong
Based upon it, he now must convince her of wrong
Against him in her judgment, must show her that through
All the days of his doubt he had ever been true
To the highest ideal of love. Could he do it?
He shrank from the question when thus he came to it.
It hurt him deep down. It revealed to him clearly
How false he had been; and for days he was nearly
Distracted between all the bitter accusals
Of conscience, the hungers of heart, the refusals
Of shame-stricken manhood, that hourly beset him.
For, turn where he would, they persistently met him,
And harassed him, pricked him, defied him to scorn
Of himself, till he wished he had never been born.

XXIX.

On departing, thus troubled, beset, from the town, —
Was it accident? — something occurred that should crown
The unhappy condition of Trent. As he rode
Through a cañon, where foaming and musical flowed
A wild torrent, he found, by the bridle-path lying,
A man who was dead, or at best appeared dying,
Alone. He lay prone on his face. In his side
Was a wound from which oozed the life-current, and dyed
His apparel. He looked like a miner, but more
Like the men who infest mining-camps to win ore
By the turn of a card, not the stroke of a pick.

To dismount, and to lift the man up, was the quick
And impetuous movement of Trent. As he laid
The limp figure again at its length in the shade
Of a pine overhanging, he gazed in its face.
It was colored with death; but there lingered a trace
Of an earlier beauty within it despite
Many traces of reckless abandon. Its white
And its haggard uplooking at Trent so deep stirred him,
He groaned, "May God help you! I can't."

                              The man heard him,
And opened his eyes. They were burning, intense,
With a haunted look in them that glad innocence
Never gives. For an instant they gleamed upon Trent
In such glaring and murderous way, that they sent
A strange fear running through him, then softened.
                                        " You're not
The sneak coward," the man weakly whispered, " who
     shot
Me, I see." And his eyes closed again. " Lift me up.
Let me drink — from your flask."
                              " Mine is only a cup
Of cold water," Trent answered : " your own, it may be,
Can the quicker revive you. I'll search you, and see
If it's empty."
                  He felt the man's pockets, and took
A canteen full of brandy from one, and the look
Of quick death passed away from the man as he drank it.
Then placing him easily there, with a blanket
To bolster him up, Trent ripped open his shirt,
And with awkward attention examined his hurt.
It was mortal : no question of that.
                                        " You are near
The next world, my poor fellow," said Trent. " Do you
     fear
To go out of this into the other? "
                                        A sneer
Curled the colorless lips.

"I was never — afraid,"
The man answered, with speech growing stronger. "I made
My mind up — long ago — that some time — I should die
In my boots. It's a trifle — too soon — by and by
Would have suited — me better, of course — but I'll go
Without flinching. A curse on the vagabond, though,
Who waylaid me!" he said, sudden energy lending
Itself to his words.

"And who was he?"

"If sending
A ball through my body prove friendship, I'll call him
My friend," he made answer. "Perdition befall him
For this!" And he moaned in his pain.

"He should stretch
A short rope for the deed he has done you, the wretch!
Was it plunder, or hate?"

"We were partners: we quarrelled,
As partners are certain to do. I had coralled
Too much — of the stock, he declared; and he swore
That unless I divided — again, he would bore
A hole into my heart. He sneaked up — at the last —
Unbeknown, and — you found me here, dying — as fast
As I could without help of the doctors."

He grew
Half facetious as strength from the brandy swift flew
Through his veins.

"Will you tell me his name? I will see
That some effort is made to arrest him."

"'Twould be
To poor purpose. No soul saw him do it. He's free
From all proof. Let him go to the Devil the way
That best pleases him."

"Is there no word I can say
For you after you're gone?"

A keen agony spread
O'er his face.

"There are none to regret me when dead.
I am friendless, — a vagabond — worthless and worse.
All my life has been simply a blight and a curse;
But I'm going out game!" And he set his lips hard,
As if battling with weakness.

"No life is so scarred
And disfigured by sin but that blessing can fall
On it through the one Life that was given for all,"
Replied Trent.

"That's the stuff of the preachers: don't preach it
To me! There's a hell for some men, and they'll
    reach it,
For all of your preaching. I'm one of them."

Pain
Of the body or soul made him wince.

He had lain
A few seconds in silence, when Trent spoke again, —

"God is father of all; and the Saviour of men
Is a brother as loving, as willing, as we
Can desire in our need. He says, 'Come unto me;'
And no limit is set to the words. Will you hear him?"

"I've long been a comrade of Death, and I fear him
Far less than the preachers. I'm growing too weak
For much talking; and yet I have something to speak.
Put the flask to my lips."
       Trent complied, with his pity
Deep moved for the man.
      "At the East, in the city
Of L——, is a woman, — my wife. You may learn
Where she lives — and her name — from my papers,
  and earn
The reward of her gratitude should you soon bring
The glad news of my death. If there be any thing
She supremely desires, it is early to know
She is truly a widow."
     Said Trent, "I will go
To her on my return to the East, and will bear
The sad message you wish."
       "It's not likely she'll wear
Any mourning," he sneered, going on as if Trent
Had not spoken. "I left her, without her consent,
Years ago. A fifth cousin of hers had been making
Too free with her beauty. I left her, forsaking
The home she had shamed. I enlisted, and soon

They reported me dead. 'Twould have been the one boon
She most wanted, — my death; but I lived, though I
    borrowed
The name of another, and though my wife sorrowed
In elegant black for the loss that was gain
To her only. I lived, and must live — that was plain,
When discharged from the army by orders my own.
I came West — on the quiet — and wrote her. Alone
Of all women and men from that time, she has known —
Me as living, and known that she never could wed,
Though a widow — in name, till again I was dead.
I have punished her so for the way she betrayed me.
Besides — for my punishment just — she has paid me
My price every year. I have lived on the sum —
She was willing to give — that I never might come
To life — there at her side."

                  Hearing this, Trent became
Even pale as the speaker. He feared for the name
Of this woman so worse than one widowed. His breath
Grew as short as the man's who lay facing his death.

"She was proud — she was handsome," the speaker
    resumed,
"And men worshipped her. Dozens — like me — have
    assumed
That she loved them — devotedly. Stranger, beware!
When the news of this day to that woman you bear:
She will win you to love her — as always she wins
When it — suits her to try.

"Ah! the daylight — begins —
To fade — early. I thought — it was morning — my
friend."

With great effort Trent spoke, —
"It is noon; but the end
Of your life may appear like the close of a day.
It is twilight for you. In the dusk let us pray
That a morning of pardon be yours." And beside
The man dying he knelt.
"O thou Saviour, who died
Between sinners, that sinners might live, see the soul
That is going to God unforgiven, and roll
Its black burden of guilt from it swiftly. Bend down
In beneficent mercy this moment, and crown
A poor life with the blessing of peace. Turn the heart
Of this sinner to penitence, Lord, thou who art
The one Master and Father of all. Make him yield
To the sweet ministration of Christ. Be revealed
To him now, in this darkness of noonday, as one
Who forgives and is kind; who is just, but whose Son
Can redeem the most fallen to thee. Let him seek
The great treasure of life at the last; and, as weak
And uncertain he gropes for it now, take his hand,
Divine Brother of men, and lead into the land
Where the weakest can never sin more."
As he faltered,
And ceased his petition, the dying face altered,

The dying lips moved, as if shaping a prayer;
And a smile settled on them, and fixed itself there.
By the wayside, Death came in his silence, and none
Could have seen his dark form in the noon of the sun;
Yet he took the life up from the clay at his feet,
And he bore it away with a motion so fleet
That the watcher knew not if it lingered, or went,
But in awe the old marvel awaited.
         As Trent
Became certain that life had gone out of the face
Growing fairer before him, he rose from the place
Where he knelt, and walked down to the torrent to lave
His hot brow in its beauty and blessing. A grave
Must be dug, and within it, perchance, he must bury
Some part of his faith in his kind. How the merry,
Mad music of waters grew sad to his ears! .
He was buffeted now by the bitterest fears
That had ever assailed him. Who *was* the man dead
In the shadow near by? And what woman had wed
Him, dishonored her vows, and such penalty paid
For her sin and his silence?
         He tenderly laid
His cloak over the figure at length, after taking
Whatever of value was on it. With aching
Expectancy, then, he sat down to make clear
In the papers before him the mystery here.
As the first revelation, he started to see
A fair portrait look out — that of Isabel Lee.

XXX.

MAJOR MELLEN to Rivermet went, as the summer
Grew long; and Miss Hope, as she met every comer,
Received him with courtesy winning and sweet
When he called.
    "I am off for a rest; and my feet
Would not carry me farther until I had tarried
To look in your face," he said warmly.
        She parried
His compliment gracefully, though she felt sure
He was thinking her changed.
      "But what makes you endure
The hot season in town?" he made question. "You show
The depression it causes. You surely should go
To the seaside."
    "I may by and by," she replied:
"I have hardly been strong enough yet;" and she sighed
In unconscious confession of weakness.
       He spoke
His regrets with more feeling than often he woke
Into speech, and she looked at him wondering. Then
She discovered his errand, and trembled.

"All men
Who have met you," he said, "must believe that you
　　never
Can sicken, or change, or grow old. You are ever
To look at them out of a face that is fair,
From your windows of life ever young. You will wear
In my sight the same smile that unceasing you wore
That brief summer I saw you at first, and before
I had come to my years of discretion."
　　　　　　　　　　　　　　　　He smiled
As if half in contempt of his past.
　　　　　　　　　　　　　　　　"I was wild
In those days," he went on, "and too wayward to win
Your respect altogether. You held it a sin
Pretty nearly, that I should declare as I did
How I loved you. You chided me then, and forbid
Me to see you again till I quite had outgrown
The hot fancy that vexed you. You gave me a stone
Of dislike when I begged for the bread that could feed me
To worthier life, — your great love. Could you need me
To-day as I need you, I'd give you the whole
Of my being, my strength, all the body and soul
That are mine. The old fancy is dead; but maturer
And stronger than that is this love that is purer
I offer you now. And I beg you be pitiful!
None of the worst, out of all the wide city full,
Need your true goodness as I do. I plead
As I never have pleaded before."

"If your need
Be so great," she made answer quite slowly and faintly,
While over her face came a look that was saintly,
"I never can meet it. I gave all I had
Long ago to another." She smiled in a sad,
Sober way that was touching to see. "You have more
Of love's riches than I. You can some time restore
Any loss of your love, you believe; but for me —
I must always love on, though my love ever be
But a grief and a bitterness."

"Say you are free
From all pledges, Miss Hope," he went on to beseech;
"Say you do not quite hate me, and then I will teach
You again to be glad and forget. I would take
You to me, though I knew you were ill with the ache
Of your love for another, believing you'd learn
In my arms to grow happy and strong, and return
All I give you."

She thanked him, with eyes growing dim,
For his charity broad.

"I am pledged but to Him
Who creates or permits every love. My one vow
Is to follow his leading in patience, and bow
To his will. He would never allow me to seek
A new happiness, till he has taught me how weak
Are affections of earth to bring happiness best.
He is giving me now a hard lesson to test
My submission to him. I must always deny

What you ask ; for no need can be greater than my
Certain duty.   Besides, it would be but a sin
Against God and ourselves for us two to begin
Wedded life, with my heart buried deep in its grave,
And your heart turned away from the Maker, who gave
It capacities great."

"Do you hate me?" he asked
With quick passion.

Her weakness was burdened and tasked
To its uttermost.

"No.   I have thought of you only
As one of my friends, — as of one who was lonely,
And so to be pitied, because he had kept
The Lord out of his life."   And she silently wept
As she said this.   "I pity you now, and I pray
Him to pity you too."

"Yet you sit there, and say
That you never will lead me to him, as you might.
If I perish at last in the pitiful fight
I have made and am making with faith, will you stand
Conscience free, when you might have laid hold of my
        hand,
And uplifted me?   *You* can believe in a God
Who is kind, though he hurt you ; you look at his rod
As a discipline : I only doubt, as I must,
Born a sceptic at best.   But to live with your trust
At my side would be next to believing, would hold me,
At least, from denial complete."

"Though you told me,"
She answered, "that, were I henceforth to deny
Your request, I should send you to ruin, still I
Should deny it. Your duty lies only on you:
You must do it, or suffer. And I must be true
To myself and the teachings of God; and these tell me
That love is essential to love: they compel me
Forever to hold myself free from a union
Where two cannot meet in the perfect communion
Of hearts, neither giving the other a measure
It cannot return, and both finding all pleasure
In giving their all. I have nothing to give.
You would fall into folly and sin, should you live,
Or attempt it, on husks of a poor toleration,
Unfed and unhelped by love's full consecration
Responding to yours. I should lead you to death,
Should I bid you to come, with no love in the breath
Of my bidding. The leading of God is far better
Than mine; for he binds with the beautiful fetter
Of love beyond changing, that never can fail."

"I would rather have your love than his."
                                She grew pale
At his wicked irreverence.
                            "Pardon the thought,
And the speaking it," quickly he said.
                                    "But you ought
To beg pardon of him," was her answer.

              He lifted
His eyebrows amusedly.
         "Some are not gifted
At praying," he parried. "I never should be."

She was hurt by his manner, and he could but see
His mistake.
     "I was mad to suppose that my need
Could win favor from you, or that passion could plead
Out of lips so irreverent ever as mine,
And not shock you. 'Twere madness and folly of
   thine,
Could I even persuade you, to trust to my keeping
The peace of your faith. I should win you to weeping
The bitterest often. And still I believe
You would help me, Miss Hope. I shall go but to grieve
That my fate is unkind." And a tenderer ring
In his tones made her pity him more.
           "I can bring
You no heart's-ease" she answered him softly, "to
   please you,
Since faith that is comfort to me cannot ease you.
I live on its blessing to-day, as may all
Who in trouble of soul to its ministry call
For relief."
     "Are you happy?" he asked her.
              The tears
On her face gave him answer.

"The Father who hears
My petition each day would not grant it, I think,
Should I ask him for happiness yet. I must drink
The whole cup that he gives me, though bitter and deep.
I may never be happy again, save in sleep
And in dreams — as I once was, I mean ; but the peace
Of obedient service may cause me to cease
Any longing for happiness lower."

        He saw
The great weariness marking her face ; and with awe
Of her faith that he never had yielded before,
He arose to depart. As he stood at the door,
He remarked, —

   "Will you grant me some leave-taking token,
To prove that I have not incurably broken
Our friendly relations? Your promise to breathe
A brief prayer for me daily would always inwreathe
Me in holy remembrance. I ask it as one,
Who, long doubting your faith, has almost now begun
To be sick of his doubt; and I ask it for sake
Of my love, that, in leaving you now, would here make
Its confession of weakness. I've tasted the sweets
Of all sinning ; I've mocked at the bitter defeats
That have mastered me. Long in my weariness, tired
Of these idle pretences, my soul has desired
With a hungry desiring some help from without.
As I came here to-day, in this pitiful doubt
Of myself, to entreat you to give me your love,

So I ask you to bear my great longing above
All the sins that beset it. I know not the way,
And I have not the words."
"I will promise to pray
That some prayer may be taught you," she said. And
    her eyes
Overflowed as she spoke. "God is near, and our cries
He can hear, though so feeble and faint that they seem
Like a breath in the night. And his help is supreme
In its blessing. You'll know it some time." And she
    smiled
Through her tears.
    "In your company faith had beguiled
Me, perhaps, to believing long since. I have fear
For my future alone. God is nearer me here
By your side than he ever will come when I go
Into ways of my choosing. I know this, and know
I shall need you forever. Good-by."
    As he went
Thus abruptly, the strength of her womanhood spent
To its uttermost, Geraldine sank to her knees,
By a sofa, half fainting.
    Through cruel degrees
She had come to a weakness so weary and worn,
That it seemed she had suffered and sorrowed and borne,
Until death would be welcome.
    Alas! had she known
How another was tempted and beaten, alone,

And unhelped of the Master, since asking had flown
From his need, she might even have begged to surrender
The burden of being.
     But God is as tender
And loving as wise. He in mercy will keep
Too much seeing from eyes that already must weep.

XXXI.

In the solitudes vast, in the wide, solemn spaces
Where mountains looked up with their reverent faces,
As if they besought benediction on all
Who were troubled of soul, lingered Trent. Of the
    gall
Of self-scorn, self-condemnings, he drank day by day
Wretched draughts. On his forehead the breezes might
    play
From white snow-peaks that yonder gleamed always in
    sight;
But he knew not the touch of their cooling delight.
He was worn; but he cared for no healing. He waited
Apart from his kind, in a gloom that was fated
To blind him to every bright presence, and stood
Face to face with dark evil, deserted of good.

There are terrible deeps that a man may go down
When his feet are not stayed. From the beautiful crown
Of some summit of gladness he sudden may sink
Into blackness of hell, with no will but to shrink
From the terror, no strength to leap upward, and hold
Himself there in the sunlight.

The shadows that rolled
Over Trent became darker and denser. The days
Moved along like a dream. The white noons, the cool
    grays
Of the evenings, the dawns with their wonderful blushes
On mountain and sky, and the marvellous hushes
That stilled all the world, — what were these in the
    strait
Of his being? Alone he confronted the great
And unknowable mysteries. Life was his own, —
To be lived amid pain ; to give up with the groan
Of an instant; to cling to, with skies like a psalm,
And the air heavy laden with peace like a balm ;
To let go at his will when tempestuous sweeps
Of the storm bore him down to these horrible deeps ;
To be sick of and scorn ; to condemn as a gift
Without blessing or worth ; to give absolute shift —
If he dare! Yes, his life was his own. What of
    death?
The one heritage truly ; the Silence that saith
To all care and all effort, " Be still ! " the one blessing
The poorest of all may be sure of possessing ;
The rest from all fever ; the peace from all pain ;
The one antidote certain for life's bitter bane ;
All humanity's right, that Divinity gave
When he peopled the earth, and permitted a grave ;
The last mystery waiting mortality's ken,
To be read by and by — why not master it, then?

What was Fame, that he cared for it? Only a speck
On the ocean to sink in it; only a fleck
In the blue far above him to fade in the sun,
And be lost. What was Right, that the race he should run
Against Wrong and be borne to the dust, but a bare
And uncertain abstraction, that puniest care
Like his own could not nourish or guard? What was
    Duty
But just a poor idol, bereft of all beauty,
That he had been worshipping blindly till now?
What was Song, that she ever could place on his brow
Any laurels to gladden him?—what but a faint
Crying-out after concord, a feeble complaint
Across echoless distance, all efforts at singing?
To yield them all up were the best, and by flinging
Himself on the Future so misty and dim,
To be rid of the Present defiant and grim.

"I have made up my mind," so he wrote to a friend,
"To go out of the world. I would walk to the end
Of my life at a step. Yes, I know you will say
Of life here. But I'm dealing with things of to-day.
They have wearied me utterly. What is the gain
To do battle forever? The victories vain
That must daily be won are but gilded defeats.
I am sick of their wearying, vanishing sweets.
There are men who will call him a coward who goes
From the work that is his to the lasting repose

Of the grave without call of the Master. I care
For no speech of the crowd. But *you* know that I dare
What the mass hold in terror. You know that I face
The unknown of the ages — the limitless space
Of the Ever-and-Ever — with courage that sees
All its possible dread. I have drunk to the lees
Of regret, and its poison has entered my soul.
How it withers and burns! How my heart and the whole
Of my riotous being are simply on fire!
I am wild with the one overcoming desire
To go out from this fever to limitless rest —
To forget — if I may!

      "Were you ever possessed
Of the devils of love? Yes, my friend, there are such.
They lay hold as with fingers of velvet: their touch
Has the blessing of paradise in it at first,
But God pity the man who has by them been cursed!
For they rend at the end like the demons of hell.
All the hope and the beauty of being, as well
As the fruit and the promise, are torn to a shred.
It were better, indeed, to be known of the dead
Than abide with demoniacs living and grim
Mid the tombs.

    "Waste no words of your pity on him
Who can feel as I feel, and can write as I write.
He has only the scorn of himself. In his sight
He is just a demoniac, rent with a rage
That no Master of demons is near to assuage

And allay.   And yet pity me, though I forbid
Any pitiful utterance !   Pity me, hid
From the pity of God by a cloud of black doubt
That makes night of my day !   I am beaten about
By a tempest unceasing.   My anchors are gone.
It is gloom without end.   I can pray for no dawn,
Since some sin of my being has smitten me dumb
Before Him who might help me, — who only could come
Into tempest so fearful, and still it.

      . . . "I wait
But some prospecting party to end the hard fate
Of this life, and begin again — where?   They will
  take
A few letters for friends, but not one that will make
Any mention of purpose like this.   My good-by
Will not burden another than you.   When I lie
Here alone in the solitude, caring no more
Whether love be a fiction, or death be a door
Into fiction more idle, they'll say I was killed
By some vagrant.   You only will know that I stilled
My heart's beating myself; and you will not contend
You are wiser than they, since you serve me as friend
With your silence.   I know I shall like the long quiet
These mountains will give me.   Their peace, when my
  riot
Of living is over, will stand me instead
Of the heaven that so blesses those happier dead
Who have waited in patience to reach it.   The Lord

Must be near me henceforth; and some meagre reward
Will be mine for the pang of my dying.
"Farewell!
The Beyond is so broad, that two never can tell
If again they will meet when they lift its dark curtain
To wander within it. This only is certain:
The devils that mock me will miss me, and I
Shall be free from *this* fever that burns me. Good-by!"

The days passed. The pain lingered. The fever
 burned hot
In his veins. He was nigh to delirium. Not
A stray miner came near where he tarried. He strolled
Up and down the green valley in dreams. He grew old
As if suns were the measure of years.
Then he made
His resolve. He would climb the tall mountain, whose
 shade
Had been over him daily; would sound from its summit
The deeps of blue distance beneath, with his plummet
Of vision; would gaze on the glory far lying
Around him, again, and find easier dying
Where heaven was the nearest.
The journey was long,
And was slow. It was helped by no snatches of song
That he once might have sung. On its earlier way
There were reaches of green, and cool shadiness lay
Like a blessing upon it; but later the steep

Became barren and rugged: for hours he must creep
Through the glare of the sun, along courses no feet
Had made easy before him. The blistering heat
Of the noon made him faint. He grew giddy and weak,
Yet he staggered along. Far above him the peak
Reared in solitude lonely. Majestic, sublime,
It awaited his coming.
                       Unconscious of time,
Save that often it seemed an eternity here
Had begun, he crept on. Through the white atmosphere
He could see other peaks lifted far to the blue
Of the sky; while the distance took boundaries new
As he slowly ascended, and range after range
In sublimity rose, till an ocean of strange
Rocky billows rolled far all around him, their tips
Only swept by the wandering, vanishing ships
Of the clouds, that before a warm breeze were adrift,
And their hues ever shifting and changing, as swift
The hot sun, the cool shadow, went by. The dark green
Of the timber-lines everywhere belted between
The light gray of the summits, and, sleeping below,
The soft green of those valleys where musical flow
The mad streams of the mountains; the glimmering
      gleams
Of white ledges shone out on the silvering beams
Of the sun, and gave light to the soberer veins
Lurking lower; and broad in the east the great plains
Rolled away from his vision, vast reaches of yellow,

Dry sod, with long swells like the sea, and a mellow
Haze marking their splendor remote.
      As he rested
At times, he looked over that ocean, so crested
With color and grandeur, half heeding how splendid
The view had become, and yet feeling befriended
And helped by its breadth. Though the fever grew hotter
And fiercer within him, and often the water
Supply that he bore was diminished, his brain
Became steadier, truer, the throbbings of pain
At his heart were less wild, and the marvellous wonder
Of being laid hold on his insight; for under
The massiveness round a great thought seemed to hide
From his vision, though dimly and vaguely descried
By some deeper sense in him. He felt that he neared
The sublimities nearest to God. It appeared
To his sensitive soul, as yet higher he climbed,
That he came where his nature the nearest sublimed
To the nature divine. He grew out of his own
Narrow bondage of life into freedom alone
He can know who is filled by a new comprehension
Of infinite fact.
     The day waned. The ascension
More rugged became. The thin air was so light,
That he panted for breath. Still above him the white
Of the peak was uplifted against the blue arch
Vaulting over, but lent him no shadow. His march
Had begun, he believed, through eternity. Slowly

He dragged himself up through the solitude holy,
As slowly the sun swung its way down the west.
The cool summit airs kissed him at last, as a guest
Who was welcome. They fanned his faint heart. They
  upbore him,
As onward he went, till he saw just before him
The crest that was highest of all.
                              When the sun
Had sunk quite to his level, his journey was done,
And he stood on the uttermost height, — a bald crown
Of gray granite, moss-covered, from which, looking
  down
Either side, he could see the dim valleys grow dimmer
As deepened the shadows, could see the peaks glimmer
With light far beyond them, could gaze on their faces,
Uplifted around through the wide, solemn spaces,
And marvel in awe.
                    "All the strength of the hills
Is His also!" he murmured. "How weak are the wills
Of His creatures! How puny the arms we outreach
In our proudest endeavor! How idle the speech
That we utter, the cries of our souls! Life is only
An atom of weakness, each atom as lonely
As if God had gone from the world."
                                    There were tears
On his face. He fell prostrate, and swift the fleet years
Passed before him as thus he lay prone. All their error,
Their failure, their loss, he beheld. With a terror

At heart that he never had known, here he faced
What he had been and was. He grew shamed and
    abased
In the presence relentless each moment. He thought
Of old Moses on Nebo, who, hungering, caught
A sweet glimpse into being the best, and then gave
It all up, with no mortal to hollow his grave.
And he said to himself, "I have seen the fair land
Where love lives in content; but I never can stand
In its gladness, or sip of its honey and peace.
This is Nebo to me. May it give me release
From the bondage of passion forever!"
                                        He lay
Thus in trouble of soul while the beautiful day
Faded out. The west crimsoned to scarlet. The bars
Which imprisoned the sun were blood-red. A few stars
Glinted down the blue deeps. The gray twilight let
    fall
A soft mantle of shadows and silence on all.

Then afar from the north came a wonderful sweep
Of black cloud that swift mounted the darkening steep
Of the summit. Far thunder growled low. The sharp
    flashes
Of lightning grew constant, and nearer the crashes
That followed them. Over the man lying there
Where the mercy of sleep had soon found him, the air
Became scintillant, gleamed with fine courses of flame,

As if fretted with fire. The whole mountain became
But a cone for electric display.
       He awoke
As the storm gathered might, and a thunder-gun spoke
Just above him with utterance awful. He sprung
To his feet. Was it hell? Had he certainly flung
Himself into a future of horrors? The gloom
Of far spaces was lurid with light, and the doom
Of dark Tartarus shrouded him. Blinded and dazed
For the instant, his brain in a whirl, as if crazed
By some terrible pressure, he stood there, and strove
To make sure that he heard but the breathings of Jove.

The mad lightning flew over the rocks of the summit
In crinkles of flame. It shot down like a plummet
Of fire through the deeps far beneath. The red flow
Of its flashes lit up the black night with a glow
Beyond color of speech. The whole atmosphere gleamed
With the fluid electric that sparkled and streamed
Round the visitor there as if mocking him, flaring
Itself in his face as if vexed at the daring
He showed, playing round him in circles that filled
All his frame with their current.
       At last, as he thrilled
To the touches of death in believing, there came
From the deep far above him a forking of flame:
A great glare flooded over the dark, and he fell
Limp and lifeless, with never a creature to tell

The wild story and sad, if forever the breath
Of his being had fled, and this silence were death.

And he lay there alone, with his white, haggard face
Looking up to the sky, neither longing nor grace
Of life marking it now ; while the pitiful rain
Beat upon it, as though to wipe out all the pain
It had known in the past. Thus he lay there alone,
Smitten down, with no time for a thought or a groan, —
Smitten down when he held a mad purpose to take
His own being up wickedly, rashly, and break
It in twain in the face of his Maker, — struck down
By the Maker himself, on the masterful crown
Of that mountain sublime, ere the deed he had done,
And the life of the future unfitly begun
By a terrible sin in the present. He lay
Thus alone till the storm spent itself, and the gray
Of the dawn in the east began flushing with day.

XXXII.

Mother Nature is kind. The cool rain pelting there
In the face of the man smitten down gave him care
That was timely and saving. It rallied him so
From the shock he had suffered. It chilled the hot glow
Of the fire in his veins. 'Twas the medicine best
For this fever that burned like a flame in his breast,
And it blest him.
     He woke as the morning grew strong
To uncover the night; he awoke with a throng
Of confused recollections besieging his brain.
At the first, all his effort and striving were vain
To recall what had happened; then slowly he came
To himself. He remembered his journey, the aim
That it had, the mad purpose that moved him, the night's
Awful vision. He shut his eyes close; but the sights
He had latest beheld were before him again.
As they burned through his eyelids, he shuddered; and
  then,
Rising up, looking out from the height, he was thrilled
By a wonderful picture.
       The tempest had stilled.
Flying mists from the summit had flown to the deeps

Lower down. The lone peak was an island: its steeps
Were encircled in fleeciness white, — a wide sea
Without motion, milk-foamy, outreaching as free
As the limitless ocean, — a sea with no sail
On its surface to hint of a haven or gale, —
A broad sea of white silence, where softly the hail
Of some sailors unseen one might fancy he heard,
Leaning over to listen.
     The air never stirred
To a breath. Far away in the east the round sun
Had rolled up from this ocean of cloud, that begun
To be silver beneath it. Across the broad sweep,
Looking straight from himself to the sun, on the sleep
Of this marvellous sea he beheld a bright shimmering,
Scintillant pathway to glory, whose glimmering
Beauty grew brighter while gazed on. Below,
Hidden under a gloomy, dense mass, with no glow
Of glad color to cheer it, green valleys lay dim
In their twilight, and waited the morning.
        For him
The warm sun had arisen in splendor that eyes
Of a mortal but seldom behold. The clear skies
Of the morning held blessings for him. The white sea,
Reaching round his calm anchorage, glistened, that he
Might be glad with the vision. For him, him alone,
The sun emptied its glory so freely, that shone
Over summit and sea. Solitary, and far
From his fellows, as ever might seem a faint star

Lost away in the wilderness spaces, he stood
There deserted of evil, alone with the good.
Here and there a gray mountain-peak rugged uplifted
Its crown, but another lone island, where drifted
No mortal along through the silence to keep
Him companionship distant. The radiant deep
Was unpeopled; its islands were desolate. He
Was alone in the world. From that wonderful sea
Of white splendor the sun had arisen to glow
For himself, as if never a mortal might know
Its bright blessing, beside, on the breadth of the earth;
For himself, as if for him the planet had birth
In the thought of the Lord, as if for him the world
Had been made, into wonderful space had been whirled,
And the Maker had set him high up on its throne,
And crowned him with glory as king of his own.

Then he saw, with a sense that was deeper than seeing,
He *felt*, the great truth, that the lines of his being
Ran always from him to his God; that in fleeing
From life he was fleeing from God; that forever
His being, God-given, ran through all endeavor
To God; that he cared for it, guarded it, held
It to uses the best and the truest; compelled
It to answer for doing or promises; knew
Lot and purpose within it, as much as if through
The long ages no mortal beside him could be,
Or had been in the past, and as much as if he

Were the one only creature of God's mighty hand,
Set to serve him as subject, and do the command
Of his will; as if God and himself peopled all
The broad universe.

     Then, as a light fell on Saul
When he rode to Damascus, convincing him swift
Of his sin, while it clearly revealed the great gift
Of his pardon, the glory that Trent beheld here
Laid before him the sin of his purpose; and clear
As the glory itself he could see how the sin
Had deluded his reason. Could penitence win
Him forgiveness? Could penitence ever beguile
The sweet mercy of God, and make certain the smile
Of compassionate pity? He sank on his knees,
A weak suppliant now: —

     "Divine Father, who sees
Every wandering soul, a poor prodigal comes
To thy table, and begs for the merciful crumbs
That his hunger can feed. See him now as he pleads
For thy pardon! Thy bounty can measure his needs,
And thy love can bestow. Let the light of thy face
Shine upon him, as here he beseeches the grace
Penitential to hallow his heart. Let him feel
The strong clasp of thy tender embraces, and heal
The deep hurts he has suffered from sinful desire.
With thy touches of cooling remove the hot fire
That his passion has kindled within him, and give
Him thy peace. Make him eager hereafter to live.

May he hold by thy gift of creation with pride
That is reverent, knowing that always the wide
And the infinite distance between him and thee
Is bridged over by infinite love. Let him see
The great glory of being, the equal and greater
Concern of a trust from the Father-Creator
Directly to him.
     " Help him now, holy God,
As again he begins the hard way to be trod
Through the world. It is dark in the valleys ; but far
Above mist, above gloom, the glad sun-glories are.
May he see them forever before him, as one
Who has stood face to face here alone with the sun,
And beheld the Lord's presence. O Master divine !
Let this morning to him be a token and sign
In his memory ever, that always above
The dim twilight of cloud glow the smiles of thy love
And thy pardon compassionate."
        Melted and broken
By feeling intense that so feebly had spoken,
His prayer became sobbing that moved him beyond
Any utterance. Over his forehead the fond
Morning breezes blew tenderly. Kneeling, he felt
Their soft kisses of cooling, until as he knelt
He grew calmer, and stronger of soul.
         Then he rose
To his feet, and looked out on the scene of repose
So magnificent round him. A vision supernal

It was, in the light that from ages eternal
Has glorified day, since the Deity spoke
It to being, and earth into splendor awoke
From its earliest night — a glad vision of peace.
The white sea, like a calm that no tempest could cease;
The lone islands outlying in silence; a rift
Here and there in the deep, through which sudden and
    swift
Could be seen a green valley in depths far below, —
A glad vision. Alas that a picture with glow
So ineffable, beauty and blessing so fair,
Should as soon fade away as the mists of the air!

He was faint with long fasting, was hungry and weak,
When with footsteps that faltered he turned from the
    peak
To begin his descent. In the valley he knew
He had food, and a horse; but he said his adieu
To the summit, in doubt if he ever could gain
What so greatly he needed. If upward had lain
The hard journey, he soon must have sunk by the
    way;
But he stumbled along down the mountain-side, gray
With the mist that he entered at length, till he stood
Underneath it, and saw it inwrap like a hood
The far height he had left. Then below the dark chill
Of its sombreness, gloomy, forbidding, he still
Sought the valley beneath.

More than once did he sink,
Overcome and exhausted with effort, and think
That he never should rise. More than once did he ask
For the strength that he had not, to finish his task.
As the valley grew nearer, more level the slope
Of the mountain became; and a lingering hope
Died away in his heart of attaining the spot
Where his camp had been made. The sun burned him, as hot
It shone down through the vanishing clouds. He grew sick
Unto death. His lips bleeding, his tongue become thick
From the thirst that beset him, he scarcely could lend
Any form to a prayer. He must walk to the end
Of his life, as it seemed, when he would not, nor seek
The one help, save in dumb aspiration. And weak
As a babe at the breast, when his feeble endeavor
Had spent itself utterly, hopeless as ever
Was babe that had never breathed hope, he sank prone
To the earth, and lay there with a pitiful moan
Faintly marking his slow and irregular breath,
Alone telling that still he was master of death.

XXXIII.

On a late autumn-day Mrs. Lee sat alone
In her room. If some part of her beauty had flown
Through long vigils of waiting, a casual glance
In her face could not show it. Some tale of romance
Mediæval lay idly before her unread,
Though its pages were open. Dumb sorrow, that shed
Only tears of repression, looked out of her eyes.
One might easily think she was hearing the cries
Of a soul in despair.
     It was mid-afternoon,
And for visits of form rather early; but soon
She was summoned below by a caller. No name
Had been given the servant, — a friend, who but came
With a message of interest: this was the word
That was brought to her. Wondering, when she had heard
What the message might be, if the effort to hear it
Would seem well repaid, and beginning to fear it
As something portentous of ill, she descended
The stairs. If her life had on calmness depended,
She could not more calm have appeared when she went
Through the drawing-room door, and saw Percival
  Trent.

He looked aged and worn, as if years had gone past
Since they parted. Some change had been wrought that
      would last
In his life, she as quickly discerned.
                              " You've been ill,
Mr. Trent," she remarked as they met, " and are still
But an invalid."
                  " Yes : I was ill in the mountains
A month," he replied ; " am in search of the fountains
Of health, now, at home."
                          " I had fears you were dead.
It is two or three summers, I think, since you said
Me a word. Were you reckless of life?"
                                        A quick pain
Made more haggard his face.
                            " I'd have counted it gain
But a little before to have died ; but I prayed
More than ever to live when it seemed I had laid
Myself down at death's door."
                              " Tell me of it," her face
Growing eager and pitying now, and the lace
On her bosom betraying the heart-beats below.

" There is little to tell. It is little I know
Of the story, at any rate. Wandering down
To my camp in the valley, from climbing the crown
Of a mountain, my strength began failing me. All
I could do by and by was to stagger and fall,

And then lie there unconscious. The next that I knew
I was lying in camp, not my own, with a true
Good Samaritan nursing me. Providence sent him
That way in the wilderness surely, and lent him
To save me. He says I had fever, and lay
On the edge of the grave for a fortnight. One day
I awoke out of sleep, and I found myself there,
As I said, in the camp of a stranger. His care
And the Lord's brought me through. When my strength
    had returned,
He came with me to Denver."
                        "He certainly earned
The undying regard of your friends," she declared,
Speaking warmly. "You cannot so early be spared
From the need of the world." And the look that she gave
Had a hungering in it.
                "I never shall crave
To go out of this being again. I have seen
How it links with the being of God, how between
The divine and the human runs ever a thought
That should glorify life."
                    It was clear he had caught
A new glimpse of the sacredness being might hold,
From his words and his tone, and she wondered.
                            "I told
A man dying," he said, "a while since, I would bear
A hard message to you. He was past any care
That could save him, — was dying alone."

                              As he spoke
Very slowly and sadly, he heard the slow stroke
Of a neighboring bell, and it seemed like a knell
For the dead.   He went on, while his utterance fell
To a low monotone, and she listened as one
Who half feared, half divined, what was coming.
                                        "His sun
Set at noon. It had been a sad life at the best.
Before going, he told me a part; and the rest
I discovered from papers of his.   He had said
I should learn his wife's name from these when he was
          dead,
And should find her."
                    The woman who listened grew pale,
But kept silence.
                "My search could not possibly fail
Of success, when, directed so plainly as here,
I found guidance."
                  He gave her a picture, — as clear
A reflection of her as she ever had faced
At the mirror; and when in her hand he had placed
The mute semblance, he waited her answer.
                                          She took
The small portrait, but offered no word.   A dumb look
Of appealing came over her face.
                                "Richard Lee
Was your husband. He died, with none near him but me,
In a cañon some miles from a camp. I sought aid

From there later, and buried him under the shade
Of a pine, where he died. In this package you'll find
The few papers he had, and his watch."
"You are kind,"
She said faintly, accepting them ; much as if saying it
Only to prelude some question, delaying it.

"No : I am cruel," he answered her sadly,
"To you and myself. I would only too gladly
Have spared you the pain of this meeting, and saved
Me the hurt it has cost. But I could not. I braved
Your distress and my own, as I must, for the sake
Of my promise to him, and because I must make
A last call upon you."
She looked up at him then,
With her eyes full of tears.
"You have come to me when
I can read you my riddle of life, can unmask
What before I have hidden ; and now will you task
Me to say a good-by that is final? I ask
For your pardon and pity. Forgive me for keeping
The truth from you so ! I am bitterly reaping
My harvest of folly."
The pain in her voice
Betrayed more than the words.
"There is left me no choice,"
He responded with feeling. "We cannot continue
To meet as if friends. I am free now to win you,

And you are as free to be won; but our ways
Must henceforth lie apart."
                        She looked at him with gaze
So intense that he trembled.
                        "What was it you learned
Of that man as he died, that so certainly turned
You away from me? What was the lie that he sealed
His lips with at the last?"
                        As she boldly appealed
To him thus, she was calmer than he. It was hard
To repeat the hard tale of a woman's life marred
As hers had been, and hard to refuse all replying
When questioned so keenly.
                        "He was not belying
You wholly. You were the man's wife?"
                        Thus he parried
Her queries, or tried to.
                        "I was. We were married
When I was a child, now it seems to me, — more
Than a lifetime ago, I could think it, — before
I at all comprehended what loving or living
Might mean; for I gave him my hand when the
        giving
Was much like the gift of a book to a friend, —
The mere thing of a moment. The saddest amend
Has been made for my careless bestowal. Ten years
He has called me his wife, — a long season of tears,
And of pain to my soul. Within less than a week

From the wedding I loathed him, — yes, loathed him;
    but, meek
As a woman, I yielded myself to his will.
He was gross in his nature, — so gross he could kill
Every sensitive feeling within me, and mock
At the murder in scorn. There are times when his
    talk
I can hear even yet, till no hell of hereafter
Could madden me so. There are times when his laughter
All devilish crazes me now, or so nearly
I wonder if reason is left me. Yes, dearly,
With price beyond any computing, I've paid
For the gift that I gave him. My girlhood was made
A dark shadow of gloom, and my womanhood knew
Only shadow and chill till you came. If I grew
To be heartless and reckless, my friend, do you wonder?
Cut off from all happy content, put asunder
From all that I craved, wedded so to the worst
In the world that is ever incarnate, and cursed
By my bondage with sin so diverse it took in
All the grosser and uglier forms, I might sin
Without adding to sorrow, I often was sure;
But I did not. I held my poor womanhood pure,
Save as soiled by its contact with him. Did he tell
You a different story?"
                    "He said that you fell
From your womanhood's purity, covered with shame
The home-altar," he answered her frankly.

            A flame
Of indignant denial burned over her cheeks.
"You believed him?" she asked. "All those pitiless
  weeks
When you said me no word, you believed me to be
A false wife? Is it so?"
         "You forget, Mrs. Lee,
That my silence was nearly the silence of death."

"I remember now," faintly she said; and her breath
Became quicker, her manner more passionate. "Did you
Believe for one moment his story? I bid you,
By all we have been to each other, and all
That we might be, to tell me!"
          "One scarcely can call
It believing, when doubt is as strong as belief,"
He made answer. "And partial believing brought grief
To me keen as you suffer at knowing that you
Could be partially doubted."
        He paused.
           "I was true
To myself and to him," she declared, "till you taught me
What loving and life might in blessing have brought me.
Imprudent and reckless at times, I confess,
I cared little for gossip and comment, and less
For the jealousy feeding on both. As for him
Who pronounced me untrue by and by — 'twas a grim
And a sickening burlesque on purity, when

He accused me of shame and dishonor. The men
And the women of brothels knew well where *he* spent
Both his time and my money.
                              "One day, Mr. Trent,
When my baby came to me," — a far-away look
In her eyes as she spoke, — " in brief gladness I took
It up into my arms, and I said to the Lord,
' Thou hast given me here what must be my reward
For the misery mine. May it minister so
To my need, I may better and worthier grow ! '
But it sickened. The dear little thing slipped away
From my clinging embrace. It was cruel to pray
It might live ; for the blood in its innocent veins
Knew the sins of its father, and carried the stains
Of his lecherous life in each drop. So he killed it
By fatal transmission. They said the Lord willed it :
I hated him then ; I have doubted him since.

"After that, Richard Lee went away. I can wince
Even yet at the pain that I felt, though, before
I had courage to force him to leave me. The more
And more freely I gave him of means, but the lower
He sank into defilement. I stopped his supplies,
And he robbed me of jewels, and pawned them. My
       cries
And my pleadings he jeered at. At length he accused me
Of shame ; " and she shuddered. " The charge but
       amused me

At first. But I had been too careless; and some,
Who professed to be friends, for the moment were dumb
In declaring belief in my purity. None
Can so hurt you as friends with their silence. The sun
Cast a shadow far darker than ever on me,
When my husband so hedged me about, I could see
No escape. Then I offered to pay Richard Lee
The full half of my annual income to go
Out of sight of me ever, and stay there; and so
He enlisted next day, having drunk enough then
To be brave. I could hardly be sorrowful when
They reported him dead; but my sorrow was deep
When he came to life later. To-day if I weep,
It will be for the loss of your love."

"I believe
In your truth and your purity both, and I grieve
That we cannot be friends in the future, except
At a distance. This passion of ours, that has swept
Through our lives like a Western tornado across
The wide prairies, may leave us with feeling of loss
And of cruel besetment. But both of us soon
Will breathe freer and purer. A calm afternoon
Of content and uplifting may come to us each
For the morning of storms. I have heard the clear speech
Of my Master appointing the way I must take,
And I enter it patiently, gladly. The ache
Of your life will be healed by and by, and the way
That you walk will be pleasant, if lonely to-day."

She smiled sadly, half bitterly.

"Prophecy drops
From your lips like a song, but unhappily stops
Too far short of a plain revelation. It yields
Me poor comfort to say that through sunshiny fields
I may go on some morrow, if pain shall have ceased,
Simply painless alone. It might give me at least
Just a hint of companionship: but there is only
One soul to mate mine; and the way must be lonely
That will not permit me to walk by your side."

"I am weak, and unworthy all love," he replied.
"I had plighted my love and my faith, ere we met,
And was true to the pledge. When my sympathy set
With your current of need, then swift passion conspired
To make league against love. All my nature was fired
With the conflict. I wrote you, I said you, no sentence
Of passionate feeling, but called for repentance
Of manhood and faith. Thus it was till my pledge
Was returned to me broken. I stood on the edge
Of dishonor, and saw myself ready to sink
Into pitiless shadow. And there, by the brink
Of that darkness that opened, shone out a great light.
I saw clearly again, and I stood in affright
At the vision so clear. Strong as ever the love
I had plighted and broken appeared, set above
Every other profession, yet shadowed by sin,
And made darker by loss. That I ever can win

My great losses once more, I may hope in some morrow,
But dare not to-day.
     "Yet to-day I may borrow
Your thought, that victorious living is better
Than happiness. Count me forever your debtor,
If slowly the thought in my life crystallizes
To character. Out of the many surprises
That wait for insnaring my weakness, I then
Shall come forth a glad victor, and happier men
Will not know such a blessing as crowns me.
      "And you —
Let me echo your thought as the final adieu
That I speak to you now, Mrs. Lee. I could never
Make certain and true any patient endeavor
Of yours: I could never prove company best
For your soul. There is only one Strength we may test
To the uttermost, knowing it never can fail:
May you find it!"
     He rose, and his cheeks were as pale
As her own when she spoke.
     "And this, then, is the end?"
She besought him with pleading.
     "Say, rather, my friend,
That this moment we make a beginning in living
Victorious," firmly he answered, and giving
His hand to her now.
     As she took it, they stood
Face to face in farewell.

"You are noble and good,
But as cruel as fate," she declared. "And my fate
Has been crueler far than the grave. I shall wait
For the kindness of that with impatient appeal,
Till it comes."
The sharp pain in her words he could feel
Keenly stabbing his heart.
"May you learn that the blessing
Of death is not one to be coveted!" pressing
Her hand between his. "May you see, as I see it,
That life has its uses and sweetness, albeit
Its crosses and losses are great!"
She grew faint
From her hunger and hurt and the steady restraint
Over self. As he saw it, he tenderly bore
Her across to a sofa, and strode to the door.

So they parted, — the woman half fainting, no word
Of good-by slipping through the white lips that had erred
In confessing a passion unduly, no token
Of bitter reproach for the words he had spoken;
The man with a sense of distrust making laggard
His self-justifyings, his face growing haggard
And pinched with the pity and torment of soul
That possessed him, — to find, if God please, the one
  goal
At the end of the world, whither every road leads
That we walk in, whatever our longing and needs.

XXXIV.

It was months before Trent became stalwart again;
But he took up his labor, and went among men,
In much bodily weakness, and often depressed,
Yet with strength of his manhood renewed.   And none
    guessed
That his life was a penitence daily; that, giving
Brave words for the true and the good, he was living
A bitter repentance for sin he had pondered
And planned; that alone in despair he had wandered
To lay down the burdens of being.   He held
His old cheeriness well before others, compelled
The good-humor that won him his friends, went about
As a light, not a shadow.   But often some doubt
Of himself sent him into the gloom that was near,
Even when he stood most in the sun; or a fear
Of the mercy of God made him weak as a child,
And despairing as one who is never beguiled
By the blessing of Christ.
                    At the first, in December's
Chill dreariness, sitting alone by the embers
He stirred to a blaze, he made offering gladly
Of Mrs. Lee's letters, then musingly, sadly,

As flickered the flames into quivering flashes
Of light, and then died, he wrote, —

ASHES TO ASHES.

A grate full and glowing: now burn every letter
    That tells of the past.
Ashes to ashes! 'Tis better, far better,
    Such love should not last.

Words half aflame with the warmth of their passion
    Will need but a spark:
Nothing remains but a film that is ashen,
    Faded, and dark.

How the fire leaps in its madness so merry,
    And kisses the lines!
Darkness will soon all their sentiment bury
    Where no one divines.

What is the past? A wild dream that has faded,
    A story soon told:
All of its sunshine to sombre is shaded,
    Its summer grown cold.

Bleak blow the winter winds down the to-morrows
    With shiver and moan.
How the grate glows with the fever it borrows
    From love that is flown!

    .   .   .   .   .

Chilly the air is; the fever is dying
    That fed the hot grate:
Out in the night the chill night-breeze is sighing
    As plaintive as fate.

Falter the flames into flickering flashes,
  Till dark is the room:
Whisper it tenderly, "Ashes to ashes!"
  Here in the gloom.

Nothing remains of a marvellous treasure
  That one day was mine, —
Passion disguised as a love beyond measure,
  And now without sign.

Nothing remains? Ah! perhaps it were better
  Were ashes the whole;
But somehow I fancy each passionate letter
  To me had a soul;

And in the dark days of my dreary Decembers
  Each soul may return,
And here in the gloom of my flickering embers
  May sacrifice burn.

No matter. Good-by to the words that were spoken
  In days that are fled!
For passion burned out, let the ashes be token,
  As dust for the dead.

So he put from his sight what he could of the past
That might trouble him, or that a shadow might cast
On his present, to prove but a shadow of hurting,
Not healing. His manhood grew stronger, asserting
Its purified purpose in patience, and leaning
More nearly each day upon God. The deep meaning
Of life became clearer and sweeter. He knew

A diviner and holier thought running through
All its uses than ever before. He was eager
With tongue and with pen for the right. To beleaguer
The wrong was henceforward his mission with zeal
More intense, and with faith more uplifted and leal.

And the time wore away. He shunned Rivermet chiefly,
Or tarried there only as needful, and briefly.
His hunger of heart for the love that he missed,
And yet knew to be his, would at seasons insist
Upon going to Geraldine straightway, and telling
Its craving of need, with insistence compelling
Anew the great gift of herself; but he waited
In patient endeavor the gift, that, belated,
Must minister unto his need, if he ever
Should know the sweet ministry more. Yet he never
Felt utterly hopeless when once he had come
Into healthier life. If to-day he were dumb,
Some to-morrow might happily gladden him, when
He could win her to hearing and trust. Until then .
He would do a man's work as he might, among men.

There are souls who walk cheerfully with us, and lift
Us to new aspirations by bountiful gift
Of their courage and hope, who are braver than those
Going forth into battle. Each day their repose
Is but peace after striving. Each day they have fought
A strong enemy hidden within, and have caught

The sweet grace of their patience from victory won
Over self. And each day the hard duty, best done,
Is this facing a foe ever present, with hope
Never yielding, and courage that always can cope
With the haunting defiance, and conquer it. Add
To the strife of to-day the remembrances mad
Of a bitter defeat in the past, the pale ghost
Of a mastery cruel, whose torment is most
In the memory yet like a prelude of hell,
And we pity the soul that from victory fell;
But we never can blame if again there be tears
And laments for a victory lost.

        Through the years'
Busy rounds, in much hope and much fearfulness, went
Up and down uncomplainingly Percival Trent.
As he labored, his love for the work best returning
True wages of labor, he slowly was earning
The prizes of fame. Without shaping his life
For the public, a place in the front of the strife
Between error and truth was forever accorded him.
Men with brave honor of manhood rewarded him
Out of their generous confidence, yielded
Him heartiest praise for the blows that he wielded
Defending the right, made him willing and strong
When unwilling and weak he became; and his song
Grew as sweet and as clear as his eloquent speech
Became braver and stronger. Its musical reach
Was as broad as the longings of men, and it thrilled

With new tenderness. Through it some mastery willed
The deep feeling of hearts, till they listened and stirred
In their stupor or pain as if touched by a word
Out of heaven. And as always the singer hears much
In his song that is lost to the many, some touch
Of divinely beneficent blessing he knew,
As he sang, that was never sent pulsating through
Any heart but his own.
     He had sweet compensation
For singing. A tender and hallowed elation
Of spirit came to him in place of depression
And pain. In his heart there was gladder possession
Than doubt and distrust. And if silent he kept,
Walking on for a day while all melody slept
In his soul with no sunshine to thrill it and wake it,
Some comfort came over his journey to make it
Less dark: the warm thanks of glad hearts he had
  cheered
Were borne to him in cheering, and life was endeared
To himself as for others he made it a gladder
And holier thing. If his song became sadder
At times than a lyric of hope, it was rare
That it had not a hope hidden under, a care
Reaching through it for others more hopeless, a thought,
Out of hunger and heartache and loneliness caught,
For some hunger of hope to make feast of.
       At times,
Ringing clear as a chime through his musical rhymes,

Came a glad *Jubilate*, — a song full of praise
For the light in the night, for the glory of days
Without shadow of dark, for the glow and the glory
Of being. And often through legend or story
Some homily ran in disguise, close akin
To the teaching of Christ, that persuasive could win
Where a plainer appeal might repel. So he preached
A wide gospel of good. So he happily reached
The closed ear of indifference often, and made
The great heart of humanity thrill as he played
On its quivering strings. So he brought to clear seeing
The secret of life, as in

BUILDING AND BEING.

The king would build, so a legend says,
The finest of all fine palaces.

He sent for St. Thomas, a builder rare,
And bade him to rear them a wonder fair.

The king's great treasure was placed at hand,
And with it the sovereign's one command, —

"Build well, O builder so good and great!
And add to the glory of my estate.

"Build well, nor spare of my wealth to show
A prouder palace than mortals know."

The king took leave of his kingdom then,
And wandered far from the haunts of men.

St. Thomas the king's great treasure spent
In worthier way than his master meant.

He clad the naked, the hungry fed,
The oil of gladness around him shed.

He blessed them all with the ample store,
As never a king's wealth blessed before.

The king came back from his journey long,
But found no grace in the happy throng

That greeted him now on his slow return,
To teach him the lesson he ought to learn.

The king came back to his well-spent gold;
But no new palace could he behold.

In terrible anger he swore, and said
That the builder's folly should cost his head.

St. Thomas in dungeon dark was cast,
Till the time for his punishment dire were passed.

Then it chanced, or the good God willed it so,
That the king's own brother in death lay low.

When four days dead, as the legend reads,
He rose to humanity's life and needs.

From sleep of the dust he strangely woke,
And thus to his brother the king he spoke: —

"I have been to Paradise, O my king!
And have heard the heavenly angels sing.

"And there I saw, by the gates of gold,
A palace finer than tongue has told;

"Its walls and towers were lifted high
In beautiful grace to the bending sky;

"Its glories, there in that radiant place,
Shone forth like a smile from the dear Lord's face.

"An angel said it was builded there
By the good St. Thomas, with love and care

"For our fellow-men, and that it should be
Thy palace of peace through eternity."

The king this vision pondered well,
Till he took St. Thomas from dungeon-cell,

And said, "O builder! he most is wise
Who buildeth ever for Paradise."

XXXV.

A GREAT audience gathered in Rivermet Hall
To hear words of reform. It was late in the fall,
And the night had the glory of winter, with less
Than its frostiness brilliant.
                           The leading address
Was to be, as a newspaper item declared,
By a man of the people, — a man who had dared
To be true to himself and all manhood, at peril
Of popular favor; who planted the sterile
And adamant wayside with seeds of the right,
And could wait for the harvest; who, until to-night,
Had not spoken for Rivermet hearing in years.
If fine irony lurked in the language for ears
Quick to catch it, the writer might well have been par-
    doned.
The wayside of life has forever been hardened
By selfishness, strewn with the rocks of dispute
And denial and error; and whoso would fruit
The good seed of the truth must be patient indeed,
If on ground that is stony he scatter his seed:
Yet all harvests of time worth the reaping have grown
From an acreage rocky where patience had strewn.

In the crowded assembly sat Geraldine, flushed
With expectancy eager; or haply she blushed
At the conscious desire that was hers. She had schooled
Her poor heart into silence, she thought; she had cooled
Its hot burnings, or smothered them so they no more
Could arouse the old fever of pain: but, before
She looked into the face of the speaker, she knew
That she waited with longing and hunger that grew
Beyond all satisfaction she ever might find.
She must love to the end, whether loving be kind
Or be cruel; must love, and be keenly alive
To her love; and no long separation could shrive
Her of loving, or bring her the absolute peace
Of unlovingness. Yet she had found a release
From the bitterest bondage of love. She had stood
In the freedom of faith, and had seen life a good
And a beautiful thing, though by sorrow beset:
In a ministry sweet she had learned to forget
Her own sorrowing need, and be glad: she had measure
Of happiness, measure of peace, in the pleasure
That grew out of daily bestowing.
       As Trent
Came before them, the air was all smitten and rent
By the storm of applause; and her pulse quicker beat
As she looked once again in his face from her seat
Near the front of the hall. He was changed. He had
  older
And manlier grown; and a careful beholder

Could see in his smile a great weariness hide, —
Not alone of the head, but the heart. The strong tide
He had buffeted long, the bold errors without,
And, within, the old struggle with passion and doubt,
Had been wearing to soul and to brain. But his speech
Held perennial freshness within it for each
Of that waiting assemblage ; and round after round
Of tumultuous cheers gave approval.

       The sound
Of his voice and the sight of his face were too much
For her fancied control over self ; and the touch
Of swift tears on her cheek brought to Geraldine shame
And distress. The keen gladness that thrilled her became
But reproaches and bitterness. Longing unrest
Was upon her, a need and a craving unguessed
Before thus she was mastered. For so to be near him
Was only half pleasure, half pain. Could she hear
  him
Once breathing her name ; could she know that he spoke it
With love undivided as faith ere he broke it, —
Ah ! then she might go from him comforted, strong,
And content in the will of the Lord. But to long
For his answering love through a distance decreed
By the wisdom of God, and to know that her need
Never met a response ; to be conscious, not merely
Of distance that held them apart, but as clearly
To feel that no cry of his heart came to hers
Through the spaces between, — ah ! the hope that defers

Maketh sick ; but the hope that is hopeless can pain
To sore agony.
    Hiding her face, and the rain
Of hot tears that ran over it, Geraldine heard
Without heeding what followed, yet melted and stirred
To the deeps of her soul by the current magnetic
That throbbed through the place. If the words were
  pathetic
That came from those lips she had kissed, she but knew it
Unconsciously. Over their meaning, and through it,
Went pulsing a thrill and a message that spoke
To her only ; that through the vast concourse awoke
No such answer as hers.
    She was dimly aware
That a gathering tempest of cheers blew the air
Into waves of approval around her again,
After silence that spoke as approvingly, when,
Far above the applause that went echoing round,
Striking sharp on the sense as a thunder of sound
Amid hushes of stillness, she heard a wild cry
With swift terror outwinging it, —
      "Fire !"
       Then to fly
Was the impulse of all. Women shrieked, and the faces
Of men became ghastly. They rose in their places,
And surged for the doors. A mad panic impended,
And death brooded grim over life, when ascended
A clarion call of command that arrested

The tumult, and forced them to hear. He who breasted
Their purpose insane stood as calm he had stood
But a moment before, and entreated them.
"Good
And brave people," he said, "the great danger to you
Is in haste; for the flames are above us. Be true
To strong manhood and womanhood now, would you live
To be strong men and women to-morrow. I'll give
You the signal when haste is imperative. None
Are in peril this moment. Pass out."
He had won
Them to reason; and, standing there steady and cool
As a master dismissing his turbulent school,
By his mightier will he restrained them.
And she
Whom he loved and who loved him, as calmly as he
Stood and looked at the crowd, little caring to go
Since he staid. She had torn off her veil, and a glow
Of excitement illumined her face, while the light
Of their tears glistened still in her eyes. The mad fright
Had not seized her, although she had seen at the first
The red flames lap the ceiling, and knew how the worst
Might appall. But she felt in his presence a glad,
Indefinable safety, that held her, and bade
Her to wait.
The crowd lessened. She lingered alone
In that part of the hall. The swift flames having flown
All along the bright fresco just over the stage,

Leaping lower, ran hissing and snapping in rage
At the man who stood under them, seeming to care
For each one but himself.   Seeing which, with a prayer
For them all, she turned toward him, as only intent
On the figures receding he seemed.
         "Mr. Trent!
You forget your own safety," she cried.
            As he turned
At her sudden appeal, close in rear of him burned
The hot breath of the blaze.   He sprang down to the
  floor,
And as quickly flew to her.
         "I saw you before,
And I saw that you waited," he answered her, speaking
With tremulous haste.   " It is time we were seeking
Safe exit.   Our ways lie together till death
Shall divide us."
       Around them the feverish breath
Of the flames became hotter and fiercer.   Without
There were shoutings and cheers; but amid all the
  doubt
That surrounded, one certainty came to them each,
Clear and sweet as the sunlight, too holy for speech,
And too happy for smiles.   As he looked in her eyes,
So she looked into his, out of patient and wise
Revelation and hope ; and love's certain assurance
Shone glad on them both with its pledge of endurance
And faith.

They were last to pass out from the smoke
That grew blinding and stifling, as after them broke
Lurid torrents of fire. In the street they were greeted
By thundering cheers that were caught and repeated
On quivering lips by the masses who waited
To see him appear.
    The great building was fated
For ruin and ashes. No effort could check
The omnivorous demons that fed on its wreck
Amid laughter demoniac, shrieking and screaming —
Mad fiends of the flames. Like a horrible dreaming
The picture became to these two as they staid
With the rest to behold it.
    At length, when there laid
But a smouldering pile sobbing up to the night,
They went slowly away.
    "So the passion whose might
Came between us burned out into ashes," he said.
"Let the dead of our yesterdays bury its dead.
You are mine for to-morrow and always ; and I
Shall be true to a love never dead till I die."

With the tenderest speech to his own she replied, —
"The past narrows to nothing. To-morrow is wide
As eternity. God, who is loving and just,
Whispers, 'Ashes to ashes, and dust unto dust,'
Over all that is gone. Let it sleep, while in trust
We walk on through the future together."

www.ingramcontent.com/pod-product-compliance
Lightning Source LLC
Chambersburg PA
CBHW030802230426
43667CB00008B/1025